AN OPEN BOOK

Revelations of a Londoner in Green Fields

by

MIKE CARTER

The author accepts full responsibility for the use
of the various individuals' names in this book,
and for his recounting of events as well
as can be remembered.

ISBN 978-179-797241-1

Independently published by
Kwizzel Publishing
86A Lynn Road,
Bayview, Auckland
New Zealand.

For Rob and Sally, with love.

Highs and lows,
tales of joy and woes.
My life
is an open book.

J.A.

AN OPEN BOOK

Prologue

Before committing myself to reading a book I skim through the first chapter. Then I read the final couple of pages and, if I discover the thing resolves itself to my satisfaction, I'll settle down to the long bit in the middle. A fair amount of time is devoted to following a plot and I don't want to end up feeling frustrated or cheated.

An autobiography is a different kettle of fish. The fact that the writer stopped sometime before his/her demise means there's more to come. So the real ending is yet to arrive which seems sort of unsatisfactory. But can there be an authentic autobiographic sequel? Miracles excluded.

Mind you, would I like to know the end of this meandering collection of half-remembered anecdotes before it was revealed naturally? Short answer, no.

So this is me at the age of eighty-two living in Mount Maunganui with Bernadette. There's a heap of water swooshed under a fair few bridges with possibly a bit more tide to arrive. You have the advantage over me. Okay, turn to the end, see if I care.

But please remember, if my memory has played tricks and this record is not accurate to the last letter, I may be watching you from above. So, my apologies right now.

Chapter One

When one attempts to describe the doings of a generation we find ourselves delving into what others may consider trivia. And so it is in this book. But a mass of trivia becomes a story; one generation follows another. This is my story: my life is an open book.

And no, I'm not going to bring ancestry into the equation; I refuse trying to prove that the genes which caused my long-dead forebears to murder/rob/plunder/command/sail/plough etc. motivate me now. I'll go back just one generation.

Dad was born in 1913 and said he remembered seeing German dirigibles floating menacingly over the London docks. About twenty years later, when he was a conscripted soldier in North Africa, I heard the sirens blare and searchlights blaze as German bombers repeated history. He and Mum were married on Feb1, 1936 and I was born on 12 September in the same year, a premature child in fact. I later worked out the significance of Mum's remark that her step-mother had told her, 'You've made your bed so now lie on it.'

1936, and the depression saw the unemployed march through London streets; Dad become treasurer of the local branch of the Labour party. An employee of the Assistance Board inspected our kitchen, found half a cabbage and determined we weren't eligible for help.

And Germany started blitz-krieging Europe along the road to World War 2.

We survived the war.

The men who'd marched the streets as 'The Unemployed' and then fought a war as conscripts, the women who had taken over their positions at home, raised a family, and wondered if they'd ever see their menfolk again, plus the women who slaved as land-girls, or worked in munition factories or served in the armed forces, overwhelmingly approved of a Welfare State. So what, that the U.S.A. thought it a step towards Socialism or Communism?

Sure, they'd stepped in with their enormous arsenal of wealth once Japan had hit Hawaii but heaps of people disliked the Americans. They rebuilt Germany as a bulwark against the USSR, and Japan as an outpost of democracy against the new China, but still demanded repayments from the debts Britain had accrued from the First World War.

We might share the same language but memories are long. I still recall the bitterness Dad's generation felt for the three years' time lag before the US entered the First World War, the US withdrawal from the League of Nations after it, the two years that it stood aloof while Europe collapsed and only Great Britain and the Commonwealth stood up against the Nazis. Sod 'em and their rant about individual freedom. The Welfare state was needed. Let's share out the goods.

So rationing continued. Dad, de-mobbed, applied for a job delivering milk from a horse-drawn cart but failed the initial test of harnessing the horse, a task he said he thought he could have improvised. Mum, who now had another son, born during the war, worked as a sweat-shop seamstress at home, was paid by the garment, and then later as a waitress at a Lyon's Corner shop. Ultimately Dad became an assistant groundsman for the Roan School for Boys' sports' ground.

Most of Dad's family had work based around the river Thames. After leaving school at fourteen, he'd qualified as a lighterman, the person who was in charge of one of the barges towed by a tug. However, transport on the river was already being replaced by road and rail. The war ended working on the river as a major source of employment.

With his intelligence and drive, Dad made a career out of groundwork, becoming head groundsman at the Roan School within two years, running a hundred acres sports centre in Southall and finally emigrating to New Zealand. Despite all his efforts to avoid politics, he became a Trade Union delegate in Pukekohe where he became head groundsman of the new rugby park.

Mum eventually bought a house over here, negotiating a four thousand dollar deal with a removal company, and had it placed on our section in Onewhero. For the first time ever she didn't have to go to work. There they lived until Dad died of a cerebral hemorrhage at the age of ninety- one and Mum died five years later, having never really recovered from the shock of his death.

That's the generation of my folks, very much in a nutshell, and they will turn up frequently in later pages.

I like to think I inherited intelligence, said modestly I hope, from my father but a sensitivity (arguable) from my mother. From them both I absorbed family values, a profound sense of honesty and fair play. Leastways, it's nice to think I did. They certainly had them.

Okay. Now for World War 2 which I experienced from the age of three until the age of eight. Acknowledging what monks say about those years, I guess they have coloured my life ever since; or at least tinted it.

Chapter Two. During World War Two

Early memories include seeing my black-suited Dad splashing water over me, a small kid in a paddling pool. That was him returning from a day trying to flog insurance. The job was purely on commission, and required him to be dressed in a business suit although this garb came from a charity-shop. I recall too, a dog, a sandy-coloured mutt, who was with me in that pool. There was Mum singing 'Mike will have a motor-car' as a lullaby. And lo, on the last Christmas before the war escalated, in a large package on top of a wardrobe was a real pedal car.

Then it was 1940 and Dad was called up, Mum and I moved into the house owned by her two sisters, Lily and Gladys; and my memories become sharper.

My maternal grandmother died when Mum was just two years old, Lily four and Gladys five. I'm not a hundred per cent that I have their ages correctly, but that's the right order of those sisters anyway. Their father re-married and had another daughter, Rhoda. This last was the apple of her-mother's eye, unlike the first three girls who were regarded as unwanted baggage that came with her new husband.

Mr Ball died after falling from his bicycle and landing under a tram. The remaining all- female house juddered along. The general air of spitefulness was added to by the second Mrs Ball's mother. Judging by my mother's comments it seems this lady, clad always in black, seemed to have spent much of her time making the lives of the first three girls miserable.

Gladys escaped into a nunnery but failed to take her final vows due to a commitment to nicotine. She sweated blood and finally graduated as a teacher, wealthy enough to subsidize her sister Lily and Lily's husband, Stanley Holmes, into buying a house. It was this house that Mum and I lived in for a month until the government decreed that mothers and their offspring should be evacuated. We couldn't take the dog with us.

Apart from Sandy the Holme's family had a Pekinese and despite the discrepancy in size both dogs played happily together. The smaller dog had in a moment of either illumination or rank stupidity reacted to an unexpected bout of affection on Uncle Stan's part by biting his nose. It wasn't popular.

Together with Lily and her daughter Judith, a year older than I was, the four of us left for Somerset. Uncle Stan, being a crane driver and thus in a reserved occupation was safe from conscription, the dogs and Aunt Glad remained in the house.

And no; nothing sinister or immoral ensued. After all, Gladys had almost become a nun and Uncle Stan was careful to avoid upsetting the establishment. He'd already blotted his books, by being one of the brown-shirted mob supporting Mosely, leader of the British National Socialist party.

In Somerset we were billeted in a house which opened directly onto the street. Early on, racing from Judith who loved nothing better than screaming at me and following up the noise with an assault involving sharp nails and tugging hair, I exited the front door too fast, and shot under the wheels of a dustcart making its slow way down the street.

Fortunately the distance between front and rear wheels was such that neither passed over me. Dusty and shaken, I was returned to the house where Mum harangued me for running away. 'Do something. Don't just run crying to me.'

And a few days later Dad arrived for his embarkation leave. He listened to my tale of woe.

'Hit her once,' he said, 'on the nose. Just once will do it.' He demonstrated. I practised. And waited for the moment Judith's fury drove her to raise her fingers and charge at me.

Look, I'm not advocating violence but (of course there's a "but"), ultimately you've got to make a stand, as a person, as a people, as a country. Try the road of reason, compromise, diplomacy but if that fails, smack 'em on the nose. And, of course, you need some preparation.

It worked with Judith. I stood my ground, ignored the flailing nails and stuck out a fist. What a reaction! She was the one who ran off to mother.

And thereafter we were friends. Just-like-that.

In the final week, before Dad left for Africa, Mum and I went up to Scotland where he was in barracks. We met the group of men who would be his mates in North Africa, in the D-day landings, in France and Germany; men he played cards with, men who shared the worries of women and children in bomb battered Britain, the temptations provided by wealthy American soldiers and airmen. Some men died, although the majority, including my father, would return.

There's a photograph of me standing between my parents. It was taken at the end of a day when we'd roamed along a track me marveling at the coins which someone dropped and which I picked up excitedly. Then I saw my father tossing one past me. Dreams of infinite wealth disappeared. But he let me keep a shilling.

And then it was kisses and tears and back, not to Somerset but to the house 44, Rochester Road, Blackheath, London SE3. The evacuees drifted back. The war had stalled. We were greeted by Aunt Glad and Uncle Stan. But not the two dogs. They had, he said, run away.

I didn't believe him. I still don't.

Uncle Stan was a funny bloke. For a Christmas present he once made me a fort with castellated walls, magnificently painted, manned with some toy lead soldiers and a couple of lead Indians.

He and Aunt Lily with Judy, emigrated to New Zealand in the early fifties but returned when Stan felt his mother needed him. His Austin Eight was the first car I ever rode in. It was a trip after the war, and I was allowed to sit in the driver's seat and push things. Dad said Stan improved in later years from the solitary recluse he'd been most of his life but to me he was generally aloof, a lonely character with a melancholy streak which he unfortunately passed on to Judith.

Chapter Three. More war years

In Aunt Glad's sitting room was a large metal cage. It was about three feet high with a sheet of steel as a roof and thick wire mesh on the sides. Judith and I slept in this. It was our indoor shelter from bomb-blast but this model was never tested. These were still the early days of the war, sirens occasionally went off, which were mostly false alarms, but I can't remember much other nocturnal activity.

One memory is of a large parcel arriving from Africa a couple of weeks before Christmas. Mum wouldn't open it until Christmas itself and when the day arrived we discovered the parcel had contained a whole variety of sweets. These were a luxury. I didn't understand why it was empty, and I was ignorant for a long time. What had happened was our Aunt Glad had opened the package earlier and eaten them all. I was given a cardboard Father Christmas carrying an empty sack and a gollywog. plus the fort and leaden soldiers.

I was sick over the cardboard Father Christmas and it dissolved but the gollywog was around for ages. We stayed about a year at Rochester Way. Somewhere along the way Mum had an enormous row with her sisters and we ran away.

Maybe this is where I learnt to enjoy tramping. We walked in the darkness without torches which we couldn't have afforded even if we'd been allowed to use them, until we reached Blackheath Railway Station.

About then I must have dozed off because the next thing I recall is a porter letting us slip through a side door because we hadn't got tickets; then we were tramping back to Rochester Way.

Dad turned up on leave. He and Mum went to the bedroom where she and I slept and Aunt Glad told me they had things to discuss. I felt hurt and deserted.

Surprisingly; I was only five, but I knew how to retaliate.

'What about that soldier who was here?' I asked after they emerged.

They both turned on me and I knew I'd been stupid. 'It was probably Uncle Jack,' I amended quickly. For many years I wondered about the scene I'd really witnessed, Mum and a figure in khaki seated at a table, talking.

'Of course it was,' said Dad.

Shortly after that we moved to 13 Osberton Road, Lee Green, where we spent the rest of the war apart from a year in Wales after the doodlebugs started to hit London.

We rented two rooms on the first storey of a two-storeyed house. It had a large garden and was one of street full of large separate houses. Behind the houses was a tall brick wall on the other side of which was a disused sports ground. A bomb landed in this early on in the war and it became a gigantic playground for the kids in the street. The wall itself was a pathway along which you could crawl unnoticed by the occupants of the surrounding houses.

Mr and Mrs Kahn owned our house. They were born in Germany and had moved to England before the First World War. They had a daughter named Kitty who was sixteen when we arrived on their door step. Sadly, Kitty gave birth to a baby two years later, which she abandoned in a telephone kiosk.

During the First World War people had smashed the Kahn's windows many times over, but by the time they took us in they were accepted just as any other couple in England. They shared our fear of German bombers, and huddled in air-raid shelters just like the rest of us, and felt the blessed relief of the shrill note proclaiming the end of a raid.

They lived in the bottom rooms of the house. On the first landing was a bathroom with a bath, the water heated by gas and governed by a coin-operated machine. It also had the loo, and the whole caboodle, which we shared with the family which occupied one room on the first storey, and the whole top floor.

To us, who had living quarters in a single small room where we cooked, washed up ate, played cards, everyone else seemed to have luxury accommodation. Our bedroom was large though, and had a single and a double bed, some bits of furniture and at one stage, after the war, a work-bench which Dad made me.

He was delighted by my gratitude as he revealed it that first Christmas after the war. Proudly he showed me the vice, a moveable stop, the channel for shavings. It had been designed and assembled in bits and from the shape, draped in paper, I'd had a fond and idiotic idea it was the piano I lusted after. So I did the 'Wow, golly, super thing' and as Mum watched us I caught her eye. I bit back tears of disappointment; I should have known better.

When Dad was de-mobbed he'd arrived with a haversack and gifts. He told me he'd brought back a musical instrument and my mind raced over the possibilities – a trumpet? Possibly more likely a pipe of sorts, maybe a mouth-organ. Out came a pair of spoons.

'The ends have been bent so you can easily bang them together. See, you can run it over your fingers and get a rattling effect.'

'Thanks, Dad.' But Mum knew what I was feeling.

I'm not particularly musical but I've learnt to enjoy playing various instruments over the years. Maybe I inherited these genes from Dad's family who used to gather round a piano in the basement of the house they lived in. After the war we'd occasionally catch a tram and visit them and afterwards return home leaving everyone happily drinking and singing. No television in those days. And the cinemas meant hideous queues.

You'd shuffle along to the pay-kiosk and then be shown in to the rear of the smoke-filled auditorium containing over a thousand seats, the upstairs circle the most expensive area. An usherette would whisper the availability of seats and, with a torch, guide you to a vacant spot.

There was always the feature film, a B movie, a cartoon and the Pathe News with the cock on its weather vane spelling the word N.E.W.S. Invariably, you'd arrive in the middle of a film. They only stopped showing at the main interval, so you had to wait a couple of hours until the part when you arrived turned up and you could then find out what that particular story was all about. Still, the interval was fun. An organ rose from a pit at the front of the cinema and we'd sing along; girls carrying trays of ice-cream or lemonade would come around, collect money and pass goods from hand to hand along the rows.

On reading this over, I must confess my memory isn't all that sharp. Maybe this was towards the end of the war as I'm pretty certain we wouldn't have afforded cinemas during it. And I don't think we had ice-cream. After the war, yes. And after the war we had Saturday morning entertainment for children. That I do remember clearly.

You paid sixpence and had two hours of shrieking, excitement. Cleaning up the theatre and preparing it for the afternoon's performance must been an enormous task.

Where was I? 13, Osberton Road, Lee Green. The war still being fought.

Dad maintained thirteen was his lucky number. His army number had a 13 in it. And that was the number of the house he lived in as a boy in Greenwich.

1943, and the tide of war had reached the stage when we could scent if not victory, then not defeat. Actually I cannot recall a moment when the thought of a German victory crossed my mind. Mum used to say a prayer with me and it would ask God to look after Dad and bring him home safe. And then she'd end by saying: 'And look after the Germans who are living the war like we are, but losing it.'

I had an idea it was significant that 'German' contained the word 'germ'.

By now I was in a permanent school, Manor Lane. Previously I'd been stuck in a class in a school where Aunt Glad was deputy principal; the only notable recollection there was of being walked back by a senior pupil after I'd crapped my trousers following a school meal, and stopping at a house, someone swilling me down, feeling humiliated and sick.

Years and years later at Onewhero, where I was teaching at a District High School in New Zealand, I swapped duties with a woman teacher. She took my place watching some senior ones swim. I said I'd stroll around the playground.

'Sir, Billy's shit himself.'

I took a breath the immediate thought being to drag Ann from the swimming area. Nah. I knew what Billy was feeling. So I followed a small boy into a classroom where Billy stood, shit running down his legs, crying his eyes out.

'Let's sort you out, young feller.'

We went into the cloak room with a long sink running the length of one wall. I picked him up, pulled off his pants and ran the tap. 'Any spare clothes?' I asked some kids who'd popped in to watch.

'Miss keeps some in a cupboard.'

17

So Billy was fixed up and started to smile before running off with his mates. I knew what he was feeling.

Chapter Four

Manor Lane was about a half hour's walk from Osberton Road and consisted of three departments. There was, the Infant School for children 5 to 7 (as well as I can remember), then primary classes for those up to the age of 11, and the mentally-handicapped section, as it was termed then, for the those with varying disabilities who didn't fit anywhere else.

In my last year at Manor Lane, as one of the elite in the top class taught by the head-mistress, I was the speaker elected to thank those of the 'special department' for a concert they'd given.

We'd been kept distant from them, and the mixture of hydrocephalics, Down syndrome, misshapen and muddled kids was a profound shock. Hydrocephalics are people with hydrocephalus (water on the brain) which gives them monstrous heads unless treated. Nevertheless the Christmas concert was a success.

'Thank you very much for inviting us to your concert. It was very good and on behalf of the Primary department of Manor Lane School thank you for letting us see it. We wish you a happy Christmas and a Happy New Year.'

And all the time I wanted to cry.

Before I owned a bike I used to walk to school, about a couple of miles with a major road to cross halfway along. Mum accompanied me to the Infant department until I had got the hang of the journey, or until she got fed up with it or even maybe her new pregnancy made her feel too tired. If a raid took place while we were out we'd been told to knock on the nearest house who'd offer us shelter. This only happened a couple of times.

More frequently I'd scan the pavement and road for bits of shrapnel shells which hadn't been absorbed by some unfortunate bomber crew during the previous night.

A raid at school was great fun. We'd have all the desks in a line which we'd sit under and we'd be passengers in a train with the teacher in front saying, 'Toot, toot. Stand clear of the doors.' We'd sway as we rattled along the rails until the all-clear blew and then it was play-time. The boys would split up into bombers and fighters. The fighters would swoop down and hurl the bombers to the ground. Rat-tat-tating. Then we'd swap roles. The fighters always won.

A chair became a superb gun platform. You put it flat on the ground, sitting on the back, the seat your control panel, the four legs the guns. And rock from side to side shooting and sometimes, but not often, roll over on one side and spiral down and down and down.

Much more fun than being a soldier running around in the hot desert, or a sailor drowning at sea.

Mum and I shared the double bed and as her pregnancy became obvious it crossed my mind that with

Dad not being around I'd had something to do with it. I was slightly worried, and extremely naive.

When the baby was due Dad was given compassionate leave and we all, for some reason or other, travelled to a hospital in Blackpool for the birth. There was a fairground doing no business and Dad gave the man in charge a sum of money for allowing me an afternoon in a small motorized boat racing around a pond.

Derek arrived. The six years' separation in ages between us meant for the next twenty years we had no interests in common. Now when we meet we're good mates but unfortunately now it's distance rather than years that separate us.

Time passed. Periodically, at nights there would be a raid. The siren would blare and occasionally we'd pile into the Anderson shelter in the garden; it was a small, dark musty concrete box with a corrugated iron roof topped with soil. It would keep occupants safe from blast. Like the air-raid shelters in the streets, a direct hit was not survivable. The subway was reasonably safe but I never went in one as we weren't near a station.

The final years of the war saw the V 1 doodlebug menace cause another major evacuation of Londoners into the country. Mum, Derek and I were sent to Wales.

The Welsh didn't want us it seemed, and we certainly didn't enjoy being there.

This was quite evident at such times when we'd move into a train compartment and conversation there quickly switched to Welsh. We discovered English friends of Aunt Gladys living in a small country village near Ruthin in North Wales. The move from a single room in a crowded house in town to a large manor surrounded by fields was a blessed relief but it didn't change my view of the Welsh.

As a six-year old I was told in no uncertain terms by the headmaster, 'You, boy; stop singing.'

This in front of the school while our class was performing at assembly. It gave me a complex about music which I've fought most of my life.

Then there were the geese, a flock of which had to be negotiated very time I used the driveway. They hissed, chased me. I suppose I shouldn't blame Wales. On the other hand the group of boys who stood with stones in their hands threatening to throw them if I didn't hand over money, were real enough.

I tossed a sixpence into the grass and fled while they fought for it.

But they were very poor. At Christmas I received an enormous number of gifts – a clock-work train set, books, and sweets. We visited a village house with the English couple who took something for the families there. For their Christmas those kids had an apple and a scarf. I felt very ashamed of the wealth of toys which had been showered on me from Dad, from grandparents, from Aunt Glad, the English couple, whose names I have completely forgotten. These other children had virtually nothing.

Years later at university I recall a group of Welsh undergraduates in the Fourth Eleven soccer team we were playing for singing a song in wonderful two, maybe three part harmony. It was a glorious sound until you listened to the lyric; one of the most obscene I've ever heard.

To me that characterized the Welsh. It wasn't until the Morales arrived in Onewhero decades later that I changed my opinion. Mike, Mel and their son David, were profoundly Welsh.

Mike Morales and I performed the John Cleese' 'Parrot skit' and I found him an hilarious companion. We've been friends for a long time, now.

I've always considered New Zealand a melting-pot where past prejudices have to be left at the custom's declaration desk. Religion, politics, race; listen, explain and argue but once you accept you're in Aotearoa, there's a covenant that says force isn't an option.

After Wales it was back to London, and Number 13 Osberton Rd again where bomb blast had cracked the front of the house, a direct hit on a couple of houses at the bottom of the road provided more play areas and of course, the old sports ground behind the house still existed in all its twisted glory of unattended space full of riotous shrubs, heaps of rubble, and wild flowers.

Chapter Five. Closing years of the war. Dad comes home

Mum, De and I returned to a London starting to scent victory. Not that we'd ever doubted it. By 1944 with the Yanks pouring supplies and men into the war, we all knew the tide had turned, even when the V2 doodle bugs popped over. I saw one – from a distance – stop suddenly in the sky before plunging down and then the cloud of debris followed by the clap of thunder. Fun, except for the poor sods it landed on. But that's life – and death- for you.

One day a convoy of lorries poured along our small back street. Dad climbed down from the leading truck, sprinted into the house gave us all a hug and then raced back. He was the NCO navigating the convoy to one of the ports.

"I know a short-cut, sir."

"Okay, corporal."

"Turn right here, sir. And just a moment, sir."

'But…."

D-day had started.

And the days flew past. At cinemas we saw the newsreels of tanks, and ruined cities and lines of German soldiers with their hands in the air. And, a sight which horrified me, men with flame-throwers driving other men from bunkers and men running engulfed in flames, rolling on the ground, running.

Cinemas... where at the end of the evening the National Anthem was played and everyone stood to attention until it had finished. And to avoid the rush to the door and the bus queue you'd try to beat the anthem by getting out while the film credits were playing. And so would everyone else and the anthem would start and you'd be standing to attention.

VE day. Victory in Europe. Many streets had celebrations. Ours didn't. There was still a war on. Japan still remained undefeated and there was a probability that the soldiers victorious in Europe would go straight into the war being fought in Asia.

Until the US unleashed the nuclear age.

And the soldiers came home.

It was wonderful having a father again, not having to rely on prayers to bring him safely home. We all went to a holiday camp on his gratuity pay, a sort of Butlins but not quite as plush. It had a pool which was icy cold. The map showed the camp on the edge of the sea but the tide went out so far that we never once even paddled in it.

I won a couple of prizes, the first for reciting a poem Dad taught me.

"I had an uncle and his name was Jim, somebody threw a tomato at him. Tomatoes are soft and they don't hurt the skin, but this one it did, it was inside a tin."

The other prize was for a sand-castle. It was nowhere as impressive as some of the others but gentle questioning on the part of the judges sorted out the ones that had received parental input. Mine hadn't.

There was a general election and the Labour Party came into power. I couldn't believe it. 'But Churchill lead us, Dad; he won the war for us.

Dad explained the politics. 'Churchill was okay at war, but the conservatives were in power before the war and look what they did for us...nothing.

The soldiers remembered the hunger marches, the despair, the unemployment. Atlee promised a Welfare State where the government would care for the poor. And so it came about.

Dad eventually became an assistant groundsman at the Roan Grammar School for Boys sports' fields. He caught a tram to and from work, quickly mastered the necessary skills so that he could put down a wicket, mark out soccer fields and athletic tracks, run a pavilion...it was a job he loved and over the years he became a knowledgeable expert on sports ground management, bringing his expertise to New Zealand and the Counties Manukau Stadium.

Meanwhile we went to the RSPCA and acquired a dog.

'Let's call her Sally,' I suggested on the way home. 'It's a proper girl's name.' So Sally became the second dog I'd ever had and the first one I really loved.

By the way, Sally is also the name of our daughter.

Dad took my education in hand. 1947 and I was in the upper class of primary school. The feared 11plus exam was upon us. Everyone took the exam which involved three papers: English, Mathematics and a General paper which included geographical, historical and intelligence questions. My Aunt Glad and Dad between them sorted out papers, made me swot, challenged me. The result determined which level of education you would receive. The top lot went to grammar school, the second tier ended up at the central schools and the bottom crowd ...we all shuddered to think what happened to them.

Before I move out of my primary years, another episode. The Oxford-Cambridge boat race was an annual affair that divided the nation into two conflicting shades of blue. For reasons I fail to remember I supported Cambridge and as the day of the race approached feelings became more and more tense until another member of the elite primary class, Joseph, and I came to a physical confrontation about the merits of the universities. A circle formed about us and encouraged us to cling, grasp and finally roll around on the ground to prove a point.

'What's this?'

At the sound of the grating voice figure of the feared teacher in charge of the class below ours, the crowd rapidly dispersed. Joseph and I clambered to our feet.'

'We....'

'I'm not interested in your explanations. Go and stand in the hall. Separately. I'll deal with you later.'

We slunk off silently. Neither of us had ever been caned and the man was a noted disciplinarian.

I still, seventy years later, remember standing in the hall, with the classrooms leading from it, Joseph at one end, I at the other, waiting for the man to come and slash us with his stick.

'Why are you two here and not in class?'

It was the principal, a thin, tall lady who taught our class.

We explained. She listened and smiled.

'Oh go to class; I'll tell Mr.... I've dealt with the matter. You can both write me a story about what you'd like to do when you leave school.'

And that was the closest I ever got to being caned in the whole of my schooling.

I like to think that she smiled because I'd said I'd supported Cambridge and she'd been educated at one of the women's colleges there.

In her capable hands we both passed high enough to merit entry into a grammar school. Joseph chose Colfe's and I never saw him again. After an interview I was selected for a place at the Roan Grammar School for Boys, a school I discovered Dad had always hoped I would attend. He'd been to a basic school in Greenwich and had shot to the top class two years before he should have but entry to the Roan Grammar School wasn't an option for him. The family couldn't afford him not to be at work.

I spent eight very happy years there.

Chapter Six. My early teenage years

September 1947 and I was among the crowd of newcomers milling apprehensively in the playground awaiting induction into secondary education. I was placed in class 3A along with another thirty boys. We were also allotted a House which would be ours while we remained at the school, which we represented in competitions and to which we were outrageously loyal. There were eight of these, Blake, Rodney, Nelson, Grenville, Collingwood, Wolfe, Drake and Raleigh. Amazing how I can still recall those names, all famous sea farers.

After a year as a member of Drake House, the number of houses were reduced to four. Drake, Rodney, Nelson and Wolfe remained. Drake was paired with Raleigh and we inherited their colour – green - while they were stuck with our name.

We wore a green blazer with the school crest, a Roan's head, on a pocket, grey short trousers, unless you were a sixth-former, socks, black shoes and a cap. On top of the cap was sewn a coloured button proclaiming your house. The button was attached by a small ring and when wearing the cap it was imperative to prevent anyone approaching too closely lest a slap on your cap caused a small but painful dent in your head.

Subjects taught included Religious Instruction, a relaxed forty minutes where pencils were sharpened and comics surreptitiously swapped. Comics, incidentally, were either strip cartoon adventures of the current film stars – Laurel and Hardy, Bud Abbott and Lou Costello, Charlie Chaplin. There were the Magnet and Gem comics, although they were more in Dad's time than mine. He kept a collection that became more and more valuable as the years rolled by, but they finally fell apart and ended up in the dustbin.

I was swept away by the thrilling exploits of Rockfist Rogan, hot fighter pilot or Wilson the super athlete performing miraculous feats in a microscopic font in the 'Champion' or 'Wizard'.

"Wilson stared at the figure approaching him, a huge gorilla-like man, smiling cruelly. Behind Wilson was a twenty-five foot gap falling down hundreds of feet into a raging torrent. Would he have the time? He swiftly paced out a twenty yard length. The figure suddenly realized what he intended and started to run."

And of course Wilson floated across the gap, letting out a cry of joy as he landed on the distant bank.

TV had just started and the first programme I ever watched was an FA cup final on a black and white screen where the colours worn by the players made them virtually indistinguishable. In actual fact although we inherited my parents TV set I've never gone out and bought one. I was going to say I wouldn't bore you with an exposition on the fatuity of TV but sod it I will.

It isn't relaxing; it's an excuse for laziness. It doesn't teach, it encourages superficial knowledge. There are some programs of merit but they are completely outnumbered by the...others.

That applies to everything with a screen except a cinema which is a legitimate entertainment of choice.

There that's got that out of the system.

The radio was master of the air – it gave us news, laughs, stories, music. I grew up chuckling at Tony Hancock's half hour, the Goons; we followed the adventures of Dick Barton, special agent and the rural activities of the Archers... sitting around the open fire in the kitchen with the radio on the table and the family rapt.

And when there wasn't the radio there was always cards. Dad taught me cribbage at an early age, otherwise we'd play whist with Mum.

Christmas's were special. Before-hand we'd make paper chains to decorate the kitchen. There'd be a tree in a bucket: as times became more bountiful we'd have sparkling strings of silver over twisted strands of crepe paper.

One Christmas when Derek was three Dad dressed up as Father Christmas. His red suit was designed from crepe paper but funds ran out so it only enclosed the front of his body. His flowing beard was cotton wool attached by a dollop of glue which dribbled into his mouth. He entered the kitchen cum living room.

Derek's eyes widened. His face became a picture of excitement, wonder and joy.

Dad presented a packet and then backed out of the room, appearing seconds later, glue still dripping down his chin, demanding who the funny man was who had passed him on the way to the toilet.

And decades later in the Onewhero pre-school, clad in a proper outfit, with a beard attached more professionally, a young New Zealand audience responded to his acting skills.

Sorry. I got side-tracked.

Eight years passed.

Once you unleash the brain the memories tumble out. I wondered how to control them but have decided it's too difficult to see any design in those years which saw me exiting the teens and becoming...well, possibly adult is an exaggeration.

Back to those happy school days. And I was lucky, they were happy. Opposite the Roan School is Greenwich Park. It has the Royal Observatory, the 0 degree line of longitude which separates the East from the West; there's the hill which overlooks Anne Boleyn's castle, where on some Sunday evenings the history of the area would be depicted in a Sound and Light presentation. There was also a deer park, as well as a flower garden where signs demanded that you kept off the grass; a line of chestnut trees the fruits of which were shaken from the branches by sticks hurled up from the ground. This led to the inevitable chase escaping the wrath of park wardens who'd much prefer to keep everyone out of the park completely.

Deck chairs could be hired near the rotunda where a band played on a Sunday evening. And there was the Royal Oak, an ancient tree protected by a ring of sharp edged metal stakes.

Rumour had it that beneath the oak a tunnel led to the castle on the edge of the Thames miles away but we never found out if that was true. One boy might have been looking to see, but in fact he'd climbed over the fence to retrieve a ball from the enclosure. Poor fellow got caught by a stake and lay dangling with it through his leg. A group of us stood watching blood spurt out and heard his whimpers of pain, grateful it wasn't us.

One of the prefects was pressing his leg, a master was called from the school and ambulance staff arrived. Miraculously Hatwell survived, recovered completely and within a few months was again playing soccer.

Initially, we were used to addressing each other and being addressed by the staff only by our surnames. However changes were on the way and within a few years of leaving school the whole education thing became infinitely less formal. Good lord, they've even got rid of flogging!

Only extreme misdeeds received the cane, administered by the school porter in the presence of the principal, a Mr Augustus Gilbert whom even the staff addressed as 'Sir', although he was 'Gussy' behind his back.

Dad saw a different side of him when he came down to the school playing field and asked Dad to siphon off a few gallons of the petrol allocated to the school tractor, for his car.

As we newcomers grew older, passing up the years through the Shell, Form Three, then the Remove, Form Five and finally the Sixth Form, the staff became more human, more approachable. We became prefects, responsible for behavior around the school, able to dispense punishment in the form of lines and detention.

One of the few thrashings I heard of involved a form Five pupil who bragged the ability to get the punishment given out by a prefect cancelled on the payment of sixpence a week.

A crude insurance which didn't last long. The fifth-former got the thrashing; the prefects involved got the sack. No, that didn't happen to our year.

We were the poor man's Public School; a grammar school the charter to which proclaimed its goal being to educate the needy and deserving in Greenwich. All the staff had degrees; even the P.E. master was told to get a degree or face dismissal. He scraped a BA in Geography and kept the PE job.

Dad, who was by now a valued member of the school staff, received many confidences. The school playing fields in Kidbrooke had two school houses bordering the grounds. There was also the pavilion which served alcohol in the evenings and week-ends when the Old Boys' teams played soccer or cricket. He knew the Old Boys who returned as staff... the sixth formers who returned as Old boys and the staff... Shag Whitten, Drip Mitchell, Hoppy Hopwood, Bob Fenton, geez, the names come back... and Skip Binnie who ran the school Scout group.

I'd been a Scout Cub when I was at Manor Lane Primary but my membership only lasted six weeks. Determined to collect as many badges as quickly as possible, I sweated blood for several Sundays at a local church pumping up the organ.

No badge but although I won a pumpkin in a church raffle I gave up organ-pumping. I dropped the pumpkin on the way home and it burst open and Mum threw it away. So much for the Cubs. I'm uncertain why these events were recalled.

Anyway, I liked Skip Binnie. He taught History in a way I enjoyed: stories recounted with humour and meaning. Above all he liked us. So I became a Scout and a seconder, then a patrol leader. I went with my parents to the Scout shop in London and was bought one of those large hats Baden-Powell wore when fighting the Boers and a khaki shirt, a scarf, garters, which kept your socks vertical and had bits of green attached. And a knife to wear on my belt.

We had a visitor to a Scout meeting once. 'May I borrow a knife?' he asked. 'Anyone got one?'

A forest of hands waved. 'Me, but it's not all that sharp.'

'A knife is no use if it's not sharp,' was the reply. And we were all chastened. Do they wear knives now? While wondering that, the thought that maybe in Florida, US they are encouraged to wear revolvers flashes into the brain. Just in case this is too obtuse a reference for anyone in the future, President Trump is in office, the rifle debate is hotting up over there and most of the world thinks he's an idiot.

I met the three Watson brothers at school – James, Chris and Michael. James, a year older than I always beat me in the 100 and 220 yards. I would win the 880. Chris was a year younger and in a different age group, Michael three years younger and relatively meaningless. The four of us tramped a couple of times by ourselves, camping out in the area around Red-hill in Surrey. It was on this hill that the four of us lay one morning in July and watched the sun rise for the last time as fellow Scouts.

It was at the Roan school that I first encountered the world of dramatics. I suppose I'd always been interested in the spoken word, especially my own – I'll say that before someone else does. A teacher at Manor Lane likened me to the line in Tennyson about the babbling brook. When I asked why her answer was: 'You go on and on forever. Look it up.'

I enjoyed poetry. I even won certificates in Spoken English, once delivering to the examiners General Montgomery's speech to the soldiers before D.Day. Dad had kept his copy of the stirring rhetoric.

Back to the Roan School. A small girl from the Roan School for Girls, which was further down Maze hill, and I were two mice introduced into the play 'Toad of Toad Hall'. Small roles, and only a brief appearance and a line each, but it was the Stage. Admittedly we're all on a stage, mainly as bit players, but the stage with curtains, wings, the prompt lurking somewhere desperately

searching for the page the actors have switched to...
That's real acting. Someone else has written the lines,
although at times when you're stuck it's interesting to see
where improvisation will lead you. And you're in a
magical world where endings are known, relationships
clear and the local audience waits hopefully for a bit of
scenery to fall on someone.

Michael Green wrote the ultimate book on the
subject of amateur dramatics. Read it. He also wrote the
ultimate books on football, rugby, sailing and golf. Not
from the view-point of the professional striving for
perfection but from the position of an amateur regretting
the impulse that made him/her accept a part in a play
that demanded rehearsals three times a week, or
struggling to survive soccer practice once a week and the
game on Saturday.

Which, of course, describes most of us.

Still, life's like that. It goes on whatever you want
or hope. You can either stand around admiring the
scenery or hove in and do something. So despite all the
temperaments, the sudden burst of adrenalin as I
suddenly realise I've stepped on stage in the wrong
scene, or the person who should have hasn't, but I know
all lines. Despite all that frustration yes, I'd likely take on a
small part somewhere if it were offered.

Dad took me to the local library and a new world
opened. He introduced me to P. G. Wodehouse, both the
books about aristocratic eccentrics and those about
public schools where the boys slept in dormitories, had
fist fights behind the gym and were all either jolly good

sports or rotten cads. And the Billy Bunter series by Frank Richards.

Another author I encountered was W.W. Jacobs whose descriptions of life on the barges working up and down the River Thames was a riot of laughter. He also wrote 'The Monkey's Paw' which as a play still terrifies audiences. And W.E. Johns with Biggles. The school also possessed a library but compared to the public library it was insignificant. The huge number of shelves, the filing systems, the scent of books and the reverent quietness. Wonderful!

So the years rolled past. Before I leave Osberton Road, a final few memories.

In the house before the bomb site further down our road lived the Hopkins' family. The head of it was a local cop whom I never saw in uniform. He had two sons, one, David, my age and one Derek's who at this stage was about six. Somehow or other David Hopkins and I got hold of two pairs of boxing gloves and after discussion decided to promote a fight between the two younger boys rather than ourselves

It took place in the bombed out sports' field on the other side of the wall which the street's gardens backed onto. We cleared a circle of bricks and in the capacity of seconds, instructed our respective lads before sending them into the middle to fight it out.

My message to my brother was based on personal knowledge. 'Go straight in and hit him on the nose.'

And as on a previous occasion with my cousin Judith, it worked. The Hopkins' boy burst into tears and ran home returning shortly with an irate mother. We saw this from a distance, not daring to show ourselves until a couple of hours had passed.

Then there was the occasion of two over weight ladies learning how to cycle. I watched the spectacle, walking backwards laughing hysterically as first one then another toppled off. Then I collided with a lamppost and cut the back of my head open.

Half of me saw the justice of this.

The bombed out house next to the Hopkins had a mulberry tree with the most luscious fruit I'd ever tasted. Not that that meant much. We had a worm infected pear tree in the garden of No 13 but apart from that I didn't know much about fruit. Most of it just wasn't available, no bananas, no citrus. I can't remember apples but I guess they must have been around. Maybe they were rationed. Most everything else was, long after the war had finished. We had a book containing pages of squares that were cut out when something was bought.

The only friend I've managed to keep from those days lived just around the corner of our street. The Mussett family owned a self-contained flat in a large house. There were two sons, Alan and his elder brother, Frank. Mr Mussett had served in the First World War ending up as a sergeant and determined to impose on his sons the strict discipline of army life. His wife held the family together. The first bike I owned was bought for from her for three pounds and even then I think we were conned. It had guards over the back spokes to prevent skirts catching in the wheel.

I think Mrs Mussett felt superior to us; her toilet paper was from magazines cut up into immaculate oblongs. Although the paper quality was superior to the newspaper we used, the shinier surface wasn't really the best for of wiping bums clean.

Neither of the sons married. Alan, who was a year older than I, developed rheumatic fever in his first year at secondary school; an illness caused by cold baths the boys were forced to take. Nevertheless, he gained a doctorate for his work in geo-physics.

Frank planned bus routes for London Transport, and in his spare time constructed model buses.

Alan's most notable research was during three years in Kenya studying magnetism in rocks. He concluded they didn't have any, a negative result which confirmed what people had suspected, he told me. On the plus side he designed an airship a model of which hovered over-night in his kitchen, a camera which took 3-D photos. He introduced me to the classic pops, Gilbert and Sullivan, and a philosophy which maintained that everything we get involved in is a lesson, albeit not always pleasant.

I'm uncertain if he is still alive. Last year I didn't receive the annual Christmas card which doesn't bode well. There was a period of four or five years when we returned the same card each Christmas, merely crossing out the name after the salutation at the end and substituting our own.

When I was twelve, we moved from Osberton Road, in Lee Green, to a block of flats in Lewisham called

Burnett House. We occupied number 19, unfortunately not Dad's favourite number but, as he pointed out and then he explained: it's a prime one.

Mum was overjoyed at having her own home with two bedrooms, kitchen, dining room, bathroom and loo separate. It was on the second storey with one more above. Some of the flats had balconies but they also paid more rent. There was a door on each level which led to a lift shaft, devoid of lift so I presume the powers had run out of cash. Each landing had three doors fronting on to it. We knew the people opposite. Mr Pamplin was the first dead person I ever saw. Dad and I helped lift him onto a bed. His son was Derek's age and they corresponded for years. But as for the people above and below, and the one next door on our landing, we scarcely had any contact.

There was a communal wash-house complete with washing machines and dryers. Leastways I think there were dryers, but I do recollect washing hanging out on balconies and in the kitchen so maybe not.

The kids all played together but certainly not on the grass. There was a bomb-site alongside our block where another block of flats was eventually built. We made it into our own cricket ground.

Dad provided the ball which he 'found' at work on the sports field and with a hunk of wood as a bat and a pile of bricks as a wicket we'd have a game. If you hit it into the road it was 'six and out'. If you lost it, you were....I dunno, no-one dared lose it. The girls played too.

In fact one of them, Brenda, took an immediate liking to Derek and they've been together ever since.

Which brings me to girls.

Chapter Seven. Later teenage years.

Apart from Judith I'd had nothing to do with girls. On one occasion in my final year at Manor Lane a couple of big, powerful and mean-looking girls pursued me into the boys' toilet demanding I return an obscene drawing of which I had no knowledge. Fortunately they believed me and it was not until later that I viewed the sketch of a big busted woman with a penis in her mouth. It was shocking and exciting but still didn't answer the question, what precisely had women down THERE. It was no use looking at statues or those fascinating photographs of bare-breasted dancers. Everyone could see and knew what men possessed but as for women, nothing. Just a hand carefully located in front of what I later discovered was a triangle of hair. Which still begged the question.

Some knowledge was gleaned from boys with sisters or elder brothers. One propounded the theory that a woman didn't need a loincloth or if she did it would be pretty small. Another came up with the startling revelation that once a month blood poured from them. This seemed curious but irrelevant. We didn't have any lessons about sex and as I dropped Science in the Remove, any chance of getting some inkling on the subject through school disappeared.

But the urge was there. Naked women appeared in my dreams, wading towards me with breasts bobbing.

I woke up sticky and worried about the process. Was it a sort of blood? You probably won't believe it but honestly, it wasn't until I was doing National Service that I discovered masturbation and that only after a somewhat embarrassing conversation with three guys in a room we shared on the RAF base at Idris in North Africa.

'Why'd'you think all the cubicles are filled with standing guys after a film?' demanded one.

Me: 'Dunno.'

'They're having a wank.'

Pause. Me: 'What's a wank?'

'Christ,' said Dave, who was a qualified electrician. He'd postponed his National Service until the finish of his apprenticeship. I'd gone straight from school and was still, despite having a girl-friend back home, a naive kid.

'Maybe no-one told him,' said Jock, another older guy.

So they did and after a film I'd join the queue awaiting an empty cubicle. Which provided relief but still no real idea of what women hid between their legs.

I met Lesley at a Labour Party Youth dance. She was full-chested, for me at the time a basic requirement and almost fourteen. I was fifteen pushing sixteen. She was the first girl-friend I ever had and I still feel mean about the way I treated her.

We didn't kiss until she was much older, and we had what was termed a platonic relationship although we did hold hands and did manage to kiss before I went overseas as a leading aircraftsman clerk in the RAF.

When I returned, we picked up where we'd left off. After six months we became engaged and certain familiarities were permitted between us, my fumblings inspired by books I'd read, films I'd seen and conversations I'd overheard. We had rows, she returned my cheap diamond ring but we patched things up and at twenty-one years of age, I was at Sheffield University promising to be true.

And at Sheffield I met Di who was unhappy with the mundanity of her home life and probably as desperate as I was to discover what sex was all about.

But before I get on to those revelations, some paragraphs about my last years as a schoolboy.

In the 1950s there were two major examinations facing secondary pupils. The first was called 'General Certificate of Education Ordinary level', taken at the end of Form 5 but not until you were 16. 'General Certificate of Education Advanced level' was taken after you'd passed the lower level, normally two years later. For some asinine reason the education authorities decreed that the cut-off age for being 16 was Sept 7. Being born on Sept 12 meant although I'd followed exactly the same curriculum as other boys in my class, I couldn't take the exams until the following year. Consequently another boy – his birthday was Sept 8 – and I went up into Form Six having to learn the sixth form work and keep up with the subjects we'd learnt in the Form Five year.

Also, to add to my problems, it had been decided (erroneously as it turned out) that as I wished to major in History at University, I'd need to have Latin. So that year in Form six was a bit of a slog. Firstly I had to keep my hand in at Form Five work - English Grammar, English Literature, Maths, Geography, History, French, German. Then I had Latin (O level)which they made me complete in one year, plus the new Sixth Form subjects – German, History, Latin (A level), and Pure Maths. This last I'd added as I'd suddenly had second thoughts about committing myself to History. The Sixth Form was divided into Six Science and Six Modern. I was in the latter.

I bet that bored you. For me school was great, at least Year one and two in Form Six. I was a prefect, a House Captain, captain of Soccer. I enjoyed History, was still in the Scouts, loved Maths although most of it was done outside the classroom, with the help of the Maths teacher who also helped run the local Scouts. He and Skip Binnie organised my academic hours. Skip also ran the Aristotelian society where we were all terribly erudite.

My third year in Form Six was a mistake. Marks in German, Maths and History improved slightly, I didn't pass A level Latin but was granted an O level, which I already had. It was disappointing. I still played soccer in the season, for the school on Saturday morning and for the Old Boys in the afternoon. But I still had found nothing available to suit me in summer.

Lesley and I would go to the Cinema. After, we'd have a major snogging session which left me a mass of still inexplicable frustrations. Or there'd be a Labour party dance. On one occasion three of us walked across Blackheath in a thick smog. Our first encounter with civilization was bumping into a bus. The conductor was groping around with his foot, one hand on the bus, searching for a kerb. We turned about and with the luck granted to the young and foolish, managed to find our way home.

Any of the family, except Mum, who couldn't whistle, when returning to the flats would look up at the windows on the third floor and whistle the tune 'Olez, I am a bandit'. I've forgotten the name of the film which inspired it.

Sally, our dog, spent the week at the school playing –fields with Dad as the powers didn't allow dogs in the flats, but he brought her home at week-ends and I'd take her for a walk up the hill and across Black heath and sometimes into Greenwich park.

At the moment, here at Mount Maunganui I have access to a small, solid French bull-dog who belongs to the lady next door. He's called Louie. Most mornings we wander across the reserve, over the main road – a doughty task as the traffic is nose to tail – and through the dunes to the beach. He sniffs every bit of sea-weed if he can find, but doesn't object to a splash in four or five inches of water. It's wonderful having a dog to walk with. I could, and often do, measure my life by the dogs I've loved. Sandy, Sally, Mash, Tess, Tosswell...and those I've semi-adopted from friends, Mungo, Titch and Sapper, Wendy... and now Louie and, come to think of it, for a glorious fortnight, Milly.

I watched a cricket match on Blackheath once where an incident worthy of a Mike Green book occurred. The fast bowler hurled down the ball which bounced awkwardly catching the wicket-keeper, crouching behind the stumps, a blow to the head. He tottered but rose to his feet. The ball rebounded from the wicket-keeper's head to the man at square-leg. Meanwhile the batters, heedless of the wicket-keeper's accident tore up the pitch seeking a bye. Square-leg, observing this hurled the ball towards the wicket-keeper who, presumably still slightly dazed, again fielded it with his head. I This time he collapsed completely and was wheeled off the pitch. I later saw him watching the game from a deck-chair so one can conclude he was not too badly damaged.

Most of my contemporaries advanced from school to University deferring their National Service until their course was finished.

National Service was of two years duration and with the cold war bringing back fears of another conflict, it had been earlier decreed that the male youth of the UK should train in one of the armed forces for that period thus providing the country with a prepared force. Deferments were available in cases where apprentice or academic courses had been granted. It was rumoured that National Service would be phased out.

I determined not to miss the opportunity and signed up.

Chapter Eight

Watching those contrail high in the blue skies over London during the war, I'd always wanted to fly. Even the huge tethered balloons swaying up there over Blackheath had their attractions. So I told the interviewer I hoped to enter the RAF and was accepted. Also because I'd passed Advanced level GCE I was potential officer material, a POM, in fact.

Our draft went by train up north to somewhere near Liverpool in late September for basic training. We were divided into groups lead by a leader and sub-leader selected by a permanently irate NCO named, appropriately we soon realized, Sergeant Devlin. He performed the task of transforming us civilians into a passable resemblance to airmen with vigour and a determination to make our lives as uncivilian as possible. Disliking all POMs on principal he appointed me, the shortest, most naïve, least likely of leaders as head airman of twenty others. He gave me an arm-band and told me I was responsible for the cleanliness of the hut we'd been given, the punctuality of the men – and I must point out most of them were older than I was. They'd mostly finished their apprenticeships and only I'd come direct from school. Also I could report defaulters to Corporal Jenkins who was the Lance-jack between me and the Sergeant.

Corporal Jenkins was a worse disciplinarian than the sergeant, largely because he'd only been in the service about four months longer than we had, having passed out from the military police course only a month earlier. Any balling-out we got was a result of the sergeant balling him out first.

I guess all the nastiness would start with some stupid prig of a pilot-officer doing his national Service direct from University casually mentioning that he's seen a bit of dust somewhere.

So we were measured up for uniforms, handed out boots, cutlery... told to polish our boots until we could see our faces in them, learnt to march in time, perform complicated about turns, cornering, plus the secret of being able to stand for long periods of time without falling over.

Actually it wasn't all that bad.

I am in favour of National Service, not necessarily military but everyone, male and female should do some form of service for this country. Could be building tracks, cleaning up messes, helping on farms, helping in hospitals. I am aware of the counter-arguments – but I feel that for at least a year from the age 18 – 19, youths should grow up knowing more about this country by being compelled to participate in a variety of activities with a variety of people. And in the process they should be taught how to handle weapons, they should all experience the rush of fear when you jump from a plane, relying on yourself to open the parachute. They should learn how to drive safely; how to sail, how to paddle a waka, experience the joy of speed or the view from the top of a mountain.

Even marching had its own attractions. Being part of a fifty-odd bunch of uniformed men tramping in unison gave a sense of power.

To organize any group into ranks and files we were first lined up in order of height. Only once in my military career did I not find myself at the end of the line. Someone was an inch shorter than I. Cor!

Then the line would be split into two and by some mathematical calculation the whole company rearranged so the shortest were in the middle and the tallest at front and rear.

Being tall was a right sod. The tallest men would be the first to march on any parade ground to mark a point from which the rest of us would form out. The bollocking they got if that was stuffed up was incredible. Being short and in the middle I felt hidden and secure.

Some men were almost incapable of swinging opposite arms and legs. They would move arm and leg forward on the same side; it would drive the NCOs nuts. We also learnt to change step while marching. And how to come to an abrupt halt without the guy behind running into the rifle on your shoulder. And how to slope arms so that the fifty rifles hit the ground simultaneously.

We graduated from marching to firing a rifle. In our last month we guarded the camp. This other guy and I were near a sort of dilapidated wire fence, looking around at dark bushes and eyeing suspiciously a large gap.

'What's that? Er... halt who goes...?'

We peered towards the noise.

'Don't be stupid wankers. Everyone uses this hole.' A corporal stepped through the gap and then helped a woman LAC through.

'Er....We were told not to.'

'Just shut up. It's okay. And point that thing somewhere else.

Incidentally we'd not got round to sliding the bolt to stick a bullet in the thingy which makes it go bang.

'Right, okay...right.' And the corporal disappeared into the night.

It was later that we discovered the IRA was pretty active about those years and it could easily have been a couple intent on more than a mere furtive bit of sex.

We also spent a couple of nights in tents sleeping on a beach as the wind tore into us and snow piled up against the canvas. And a map-reading exercise the team I was leading would have been won but my team included two slow-speaking men from Somerset. I'd cut a corner, probably illegally but it had put us way ahead of the rest. My Somerset men refused to walk any faster than their speech.

'T'ain't no use, boyer, we bain't be hurrying .

So we were overtaken.

The weekly hut inspections were traumatic. We stood rigidly at the foot of our respective beds while Sergeant Devlin, followed by the lance-corporal, closely studied the alignments of bedding and beds, rubbed a finger along shelves and eyed savagely the curling smoke from a cigarette that some idiot had chucked into the waste bin without stubbing out. Horror. And another night of polishing for a repeat performance the following day.

We progressed through the weeks, became the senior in-take, and were interviewed for our trade.

' 2772890 AC2 Carter, Sir.'

'Wie geht's tu?'

'Er...'

God, what on earth was he talking about?

'I thought you knew German.'

'Ah, er, yes. It's been some time.'

So I didn't get accepted as an interpreter.

Finally I departed for a week's leave spent with Lesley, and the folks, and taking Sally for walks. Then I disappeared again, this time to a base just outside the Black Hills of North Wales where I learnt the skills necessary to become a progress clerk.

RAF was a doddle compared to basic training. Admittedly we still had to keep ourselves and equipment neat and clean and we were marched to and from lessons. But the whole affair was relaxed, similar to school but we were paid for attending. That was the thing. Apart from a paper round which earned me half a crown a week and entailed arising at 5.30 am to be at the newsagent's at 5.45 to complete the round by 7 etc...I'd never worked for money, let alone worked full-time.

We'd be called into the parade are and one by one called up to the pay-officer.

'AC2 Carter 2772890, Sir.'

Handed an envelope and then go around to the Naafi to buy a cup of tea and a bun. Despite its cheapness on base it wasn't until long after National Service that I learned to appreciate beer.

We'd always enjoyed a glass of cider at home on Sundays. It was a special treat given almost ceremonial reverence. There'd always be a drop left over for someone to finish off on Monday.

One week I had the, to me hilarious, idea of swigging that last drop and replacing it with vinegar. T following Monday I awaited Dad's arrival. He took the customary swig but didn't turn a hair.

'I'll let you finish this, Mike.' He handed me the bottle with a genial smile.

Well, honour was at stake. I finished it off.

'Great!'

Then we both laughed.

Along with the cider, Sunday dinner was always roast of some sort and vegies. One Sunday for some forgotten reason I pushed it to one side. Maybe it was the greens, maybe just pre- teen hormones.

'Don't want this,' I said.

'If you don't want it, Sally will,' said my mother.

'Huh.' I left the table and headed for the door.

'Where're you going?'

'Out.'

An hour later I buried my pride, returned home, sighed. 'All right, I'll eat it.'

'You're too late. I gave it to Sally.

And Sally looked up, her tail slowly wagging.

Back to Trade training.

Someone remembered how to change step. Left, right, left, right left, left skip, left.' Then we perfected performing this to a Colonel Bogey march changing step when the line, 'only one ball' finished.

There was one NCO who obviously enjoyed marching his classes to lessons. He would lineup his men in ranks of four. Then:

'By the left, quick march. Left right left right.

Obediently and smartly we would follow him striding in front of us as he periodically called out the cadence. 'Left, right, left right.'

Someone would whistle softly down the line. And the NCO to his horror would find himself out of step with his men. We learned how to colour in bar graphs so offices would look attractive; we were reminded of our O level statistics; we were shown typewriters but training didn't include lessons. We did learn how to make carbon copies of graphs, sometimes five at a time. No fancy copiers or computers in those days.

I spent a week-end in the Black Hills camping high up amongst the heather above tiny villages. When I returned our intake was asked about preferred postings. I asked for one overseas and to my surprise and pleasure got one to RAF Idris a base in North Africa just outside of Tripoli. I didn't tell Lesley I'd asked for the overseas posting. I felt rotten about this but managed to overcome the feeling and two weeks later we parted with promises of letters and loyalty.

Chapter Nine. RAF Idris. 1956 - 1957

A plane-load of us flew out to the Tripoli base, stopping at Rome to refuel. I felt sick most of the trip and vomited twice. It just about stuffed up any ideas I'd ever felt about flying. There's the start of a head-ache, a sweaty gloss to the face, a nasty taste in the throat. Then the stomach heaves.... There are pills you can take and for years I'd always dose myself before flying. Then jet planes started flying people, flying above turbulence. Wonderful. But years ahead.

Anyway, I tottered to the ground at Idris and was delivered to a block of twenty rooms over-looking a courtyard. There I was introduced to Jock and Don and Jack, my room-mates for the next year. None of them had come straight from school. They looked on me as a sort of novitiate they were responsible for introducing into the modern world.

I was very lucky to have the companionship of the guys I met in the RAF.

When I reflect on that year and a half in Idris, I realize how much it influenced the rest of my life. Many of my school contemporaries went directly to tertiary education and quite a number didn't finish the course. National Service completed my boyhood.

The base acted as a stop-over for planes. Here they would be re-fuelled and serviced. There was a station Anson – a plane capable of transporting an athletic team over to Malta, and an AOP (Air Observation Plane). This was a two-seated plane termed an Auster. I don't know what it was supposed to spot but it was piloted by a Flight Lieutenant who was also the officer in charge of the athletic team and he let me accompany him a couple of times.

As the flight was of a short duration I managed not to be sick.

I worked in the Daily Servicing Section, termed the DSS and was responsible, under a corporal, for the records of work on the various planes that dropped in. Our whole section was run by a Squadron Leader and the inferior complex in me didn't quite know how to take him. My own London accent has stayed with me all my life despite fifty odd years in New Zealand and in those days the British Broadcasting Corporation accent was the one cultivated by the governing classes of whom I felt myself definitely beneath. It was refreshing but surprising to hear pure cockney issuing from the lips of our Squadron Leader.

It was he who virtually compelled me to take on University when I was dithering about remaining in the RAF after my time there drew to a close.

For most of the base, work started at 0700 before the heat became unbearable – at one time it was a blazing 50 degrees – and would finish about 1400 and then we disappeared into our rooms until dinner time at 1800. That was the system for the first few months after my arrival except that I discovered there was a sailing club in Tripoli and a gharry (lorry) that would convey anyone wanting to get into the city for free, and collect them in time for dinner. You could even, if you chatted up the cooks, have a later meal kept for you. Life was lazy, sweet and a gentle spirit of peace pervaded the whole camp.

And then the CO left; a new one arrived, intent on bringing life, purpose, drive and discipline to the scene. Rumour had it he had been incarcerated in a POW camp for three years after being shot down over Germany and he felt the men – and officers – needed jolting out of their sense of serenity.

He called everyone together in a hangar.

'You are stationed on a base which is essentially a garage for planes. It is a responsible duty but you are all relatively safe. In other armed forces, the Army, the Navy, men in the ranks share the dangers of their officers. The RAF is different. Most of the dangers involved in flying are faced by officers. I feel that this has given rise to a sense of complacency on this base.'

I looked around. It was totally the wrong thing to say. There were NCOs here who never flew, but knew that the planes depended on them. There were corporals who'd re-enlisted after the war who were wearing the half-wings of an AG. It was a speech I didn't think the base deserved.

'There are going to be changes. I want to see this base come alive. There will be a full station inspection once a week for everyone except those on essential duties. Every Monday morning until further notice each section will supply the station Warrant Officer with two men for general duties. In return for a new spirit, a cleaner base, a sharper, more vibrant approach on your parts, I am instituting evening entertainments where you can experience the variety of skills I am sure you all possess. Also a station magazine. Thank you.'

It antagonized many people but as far as I was concerned had no real impact. When it comes to the crunch one man can't beat the mob. Although that's a bit daft. History is littered with people who controlled mobs.

We had our inspection.

The C.O marched along our lines stopping at various times to look at buttons.

'This Airman's brass is dirty. Get his name sergeant and he can report to the Station Warrant Officer tomorrow morning.'

'LAC Carter,' I muttered looking straight ahead. As I am only a couple of inches over five feet anyone trying to catch my eye had to bend down, or stand back a couple of yards. It was another occasion when lack of height was of benefit. Dad said his foxhole was always dug quicker than anyone else's because there was less of him to hide.

The following morning I reported to the SWO. 'Why are you here, Carter?' he asked. I knew him vaguely from the Tripoli Dolphin Force's Sailing club which I'd joined.

'CO said I had dirty buttons, sir.'

'He said the same about mine. Give 'em a polish, lad. Dismiss.'

The other innovation was reporting for general duties. I got clobbered for them as the recording office of DSS was the least important part of its business of keeping the planes in the air. They couldn't spare mechanics or engineers but form-fillers were expendable. I met up with another clerk and we were handed pots of black and white paint and told to use them on the stones outside the admin block.

'You start at one end with the white, I'll start at the other with the black . Do 'em alternately. This way we'll keep out of each other's way.'

As he seemed knowledgeable and was an SAC I followed his instructions. We met in the middle both claiming the middle stone. Fortunately it was a hot day, the white dried quickly and were hastily repainted.

The following Monday when we reported, the SWO had five pairs of men on general duties. He looked a bit bothered and I had an idea.

'If there's nothing really important, sir, there's a boat need repainting.'

'Go and bloody do it then. Get the equipment from stores.'

Four of us regularly took the Gharry into Tripoli to sail at the Forces Club. There were Fireflies, a cold moulded plywood 12 foot dinghy which was restricted to the experts and a heavy 14footer called Snipes. A sergeant had found a couple of the latter class on our base, and had restored one. He'd taken it down to the club-house and moored it out in the harbour.

'Where is it?' I asked when he met up with us one afternoon.

'Out there ....'

One of the two soldiers whose duty it was to look after the club's boats, a cushy number if ever there was one, sauntered over.

'Sorry sarge, it sank.'

And there it was, in twenty feet of water.

We left the sergeant discussing how it could be raised but the point of the anecdote is that in the process we'd been told of a sixteen footer with a metal hull also in a shed on base.

It was this we were given permission to work on, which filled in the following few Mondays nicely. The SWO (Station Warrant Officer) was grateful not to have airman skulking around filling in time, we were happy scraping down and painting a boat we ultimately had great fun with, and the CO, if ever he heard about our "general duties" could see we were happily and productively employed.

Talking of the CO, he regularly flew the Anson and when it was up for its regular service he discovered it needed a new instrument. This was duly ordered and after, a couple of weeks with the CO becoming more and more agitated about his loss of air-hours, it arrived.

And while a fitter was removing the defunct instrument a tractor ran over the replacement instrument and totally destroyed it.

All in DSS walked a very, very careful line for the next month.

Back to the boat.

Jock who was also a member of the yacht club, had managed to get on the general duties roster and the pair of us conned the paint storeman to provide us with the necessary equipment to remove the old paint and slap another one on.

'You can have the burners and a scraper,' the paint-expert told us, 'or a chemical you spread on that lifts the old paint so you just wipe it off.'

'We'll take both,' said Jock. He was older than I and spoke with assurance. 'What do you want to do?'

'I'll have the flame-thrower,' I replied. 'Looks like fun.' And indeed it was –admittedly not as quick as slapping on a chemical as Jock was doing – but had an air of adventure about it, sapping the paint with a blow-torch and scraping.

Jock reached the bow of the boat and started down my side.

'Beat ya!'

And then the flame reached a blob of chemical, there was a loud 'woof' and the boat was on fire.

Luckily it was a metal hull.

The station fire brigade raced up ready to spray anyone and anything but we convinced them it was a controlled scrape and they didn't have to report a dangerous fire threatening the base. They watched as the paint burnt off and the flames died and we nonchalantly scraped off blackened bits of boat.

We had heaps of fun in that boat which we named 'Angeline'. We sailed out of Tripoli harbour and headed down the coast to a small Arab village where there was a tuna factory. The first time we camped on the sand there, was a weekend. We'd raced off one Friday afternoon in the blazing sun having acquired food for the weekend. There was no fresh milk anywhere around the base so we were given tins of evaporated milk. I loved the stuff.

We left our uniforms at the sailing club and set off wearing just shorts. I don't think we even had life-jackets.

Certainly we'd forgotten blankets, shirts, let alone washing-gear. We'd also forgotten how cold the nights were.

That night the five of us lay on the sands shivering under the main sail and the jib.

Still, the sun shone from an early hour and the sea was red with blood. The Arabs had a school of eight foot tuna trapped in a large net and were killing them with large gaffs. The tuna were dragged ashore and the water slowly cleared. Jordan, one of our team, donned some scuba gear and pottered off for a morning swim. Suddenly someone pointed out the fin.

'Maybe we should warn him.'

Geordie swam lazily swam up and down the beach.

The shark, obviously attracted by the residual bits of tuna, drew closer.

We shouted. Geordie's snorkel stuck up out of the water as he scanned the depths beneath him oblivious of the menace close by.

Maybe Geordie didn't smell right. He returned to land unscathed and was quite annoyed when we pointed out the fin.

The end of the story had the shark approach within two metres of the shore and a couple of Arabs waded in and plunged great gaffs into its body and dragged it thrashing onto the beach.

Poor old shark. When I see people haul fish out of their element by a hook I feel that anything the shark does is justified. I know it's hypocritical, think fish'n chips, and so's my attitude to meat, in so far as I hate to think of the animals slaughtered yet still enjoy a tender steak. But why blacken the character of the shark, why call them killer-sharks? If any species deserves the name 'killer' it's the human and most of it's sheer recreational murder. I feel a smart comment about the gun lobby in the United States could be made here but I'll let that rest for now.

Sailing was one of the principal skills I learned in the RAF. Another was acquired if not mastered, in conjunction with it. That was hanging out over a beer. When we had finished our basic training we congregated at the local pub.

'I don't like beer,' I confessed after being bought a half of ale.

'I know what you'll like,' said Ginger who'd wanted me to ditch the two Somerset men on our expedition. He'd run off ahead, been the first one back and felt guilty that he'd deserted me. 'Try this.' And gave me a Drambuie, a sweetish soporific which was certainly an improvement on beer.

As I said, prior to that my only association with alcohol had been a bottle of cider each Sunday. At the Tripoli Dolphin Services Yacht Club on a Saturday night the RAF Idris contingent would wait around until all the Army mob, mostly officers. They didn't really know how to cope with us self-confident RAF berks who recognised bullshit and could handle a sailing dinghy as well as any of them, had left.

Then the two lance-corporals who looked after the boats and buildings would open the bar (again) and we'd sit around and chat and drink before bunking down in the clubhouse until the following day when they'd be more racing.

And someone introduced me to Tom Collins, whisky with bitters, lime and lemonade; and John Collins ditto but with a gin base. And that, until I came to New Zealand and discovered ice-cold beer, was my alcohol of choice for ages.

There were two men who taught me the joys of sailing a dinghy.

Johnny was a civil engineer who had a negative handicap of over a minute. That meant that at the end of a race, a minute was added to his recorded finishing time. To win a race he'd have to finish at least a minute ahead of the fleet. He accepted me as a crew because no-one else would sit in the same dinghy with him.

'Just sit,' he told me the first time I stepped into his Fire-fly. 'Don't touch anything. Do what you're told.' He steered, controlled the main and held the jib-sheets. 'Lean out. Get in. Lie down on the foredeck.'

I quickly realised I was just ballast.

It seemed his wife had crewed for him for the almost six months before she resigned position as crew and wife. One of the rules of the class was that a race must finish with the same number of people in the dinghy as it held at the start. On the final race of the previous season, as Johnny neared the line, over two minutes ahead of anyone else, his wife had said, 'Sod you and your sailing.'

Then she jumped overboard and swam ashore.

I learnt then to be aware that the slightest change in the wind meant readjusting the sails. I learnt that to jump up onto a plane, the old equivalent of today's foiling, meant exquisite judgement. To win meant attention to detail.

Johnny went back to England for a month and I crewed with Mr Goldworthy, a gentleman considerably older than Johnny who just enjoyed sailing. Winning was not the main consideration.

So basically, for me racing's fun, and why race if you don't intend to win? But racing and sailing are different things. On the other hand, it's good to feel you're getting the best out of a boat. So I'd yell and shout as we came into shore. 'Rob, stand by anchor. Sally, look after the main, let it down when I say. Di, point up to wind a bit. Get ready to stick her into wind. I'll look after the centre-board. Right now Di, into wind; don't go about; hold it. Okay Sally, let go the main. Wait till we stop, Rob. Now, let go anchor.'

The family would tell me to calm down. I'd take a deep breath and do my best. Both Rob and Sally say they are surprised Di and I stayed married until death did us part.

Two Arab gentlemen seated peacefully in their rowing boat a couple of hundred metres off-shore, yelled in horror as we swooshed down upon them. 'Mad, fucking Englishman.'

Hell! An empty horizon for miles, and the entire Mediterranean Sea to sail in, we'd almost caused an international incident. As it was we had to free a fishing line apologetically from our rudder all the while abuse being hurled at us.

It was a warm night with a full moon. We glided in our dinghies helped by a gentle breeze past brightly lit restaurants filled with glamourous patrons and romantic Italian music. It was a night race and pure magic. I cannot remember anything else about it except for the lights, the music, soft air and sailing.

The first time I was officer-of-the-day in charge of a club race was not magic. As, I've mentioned, apart from the RAF, club members were commissioned officers. That we had to take our turn at being OoD (Officer of the Day) was a surprise.

I was given as assistant, the daughter of a Captain, and we managed the start perfectly; the five minute bell, the two minute, the start. No infringements. The problem came at the end of the race when I had to record the time each person finished, to the nearest second and then add or subtract the various handicaps and come up with a winner.

The first one across was something like 45 mins 23 sec. (This is merely an example. I can't remember the exact time after sixty or so years). The daughter recorded the time. Then the fleet bunched up. To expedite the process I started omitting the minute element, relying on my assistant to put in the minute side. The final dinghy crossed the finishing line about 7 minutes after the first.

I was handed a list of which only the first and last had the minutes alongside them.

Rather than admit a blunder, I sent my assistant away. Using a good deal of guess-work, a knowledge of who ought to have come first, and appreciating that what <u>really mattered</u> was a confident presentation of the results, I added, subtracted, and codged numbers, until everyone had the position in which he'd crossed the line with a time which corresponding to that position. This differed from reality by up to 'God-knows' how many minutes.

The final time derived from the handicap was a load of old bollocks as they say.

No-one mentioned any discrepancy but the keen ones who always took a watch must have wondered.

Once we took the RAF Idris Education officer for a ride in Angeline. He was asked to be put ashore somewhere inside the harbour after half an hour complaining of sea-sickness and walked back.

I contacted the education officer when I realised I'd sooner be a park ranger than a teacher. The officer said I'd need chemistry at A level so I signed up for an O level course blithely thinking I'd knock them both off before I left Idris. It took six weeks before I appreciated the error of my ways. After all, I was the one who when asked by my Form Four Science teacher at school what a base was (a soluble alkali if you're interested) who'd answered that it was the bottom of something.

I chose therefore to take my SAC (Senior Aircraftsman) exam and sewed on my badge of propellers a few months later, also collecting a few shillings extra in my pay-packet.

Months drifted by. The station drama club produced a comedy entitled 'A horse, a horse.' It was directed by one of the cooks and included in its cast the CO's wife, a pilot officer from admin. and a couple of berks besides me. That was a fair mix but we all worked together and it was fun.

The P.O. like most of us was a National Service conscript, and was as unsure of himself as we were. On one occasion during a billet cleaning session when he hove up to inspect, we were in the process of throwing buckets of water over everything and everyone. He took one look at the situation and fled. Later he told us rather shyly how the commissioned ranks had tossed cups of water at each other.

The memories flood back.

With the Anson again flyable the CO took the athletic team to a Group competition in Malta. I ran the 880yd leg of a relay consisting of a starting leg of 100yds, then 440, then 880 and finishing with a 220. We won. We should have gone on a boozy celebration in 'The Gut' where women provided live and unusual entertainment but the long jumper had arranged a meeting with someone in Valhetta who had done something underhand at a previous base in England. He wanted a witness.

'You wouldn't like the Gut,' said the long-jumper. 'It's pretty foul.'

So that idea went west; and instead I listened to a long rambling conversation about something to do with spare parts. He got time in a military prison in any case without me being called.

Jack and I also visited Malta on our way to Italy where we spent our leave. Jack was as innocent and naïve as I was so the delights and mysteries of the 'Gut' were by-passed. We weren't allowed in St Peter's because we were wearing shorts; we did pop in to various cathedrals in Florence and Venice; and we looked disparagingly at heaps of ancient history. We visited the coliseum and all that old stuff. Remember, I was only nineteen. Doubtless later I would've enjoyed exploring the beginnings of civilization. At the time I could only think that the bombed-out houses I'd seen during the war seemed more real.

Then we reached Como.

We tramped through the lower hills beneath the distant mountains. At nights we slept in a Youth Hostel overlooking the lake. Once we met up with a group of shepherds and joined them around a fire sharing their bottles of wine and I felt that here at least was part of Italy I could love.

Most of the way north we'd hitchhiked, quite successfully. On the return our last lift was on the back of a truck carrying bags of flour. In Naples we climbed down covered in flour.

Took ages to remove the last traces. No cars stopped and even a bus-driver was a bit dubious when he saw us at the terminus.

There were times I needed reminding of home. My parents wrote regularly but the letters from Lesley were sporadic. Truly, thinking back on it I can't blame her. But at the time, seeing other guys getting letters from their girlfriends, I'd wait desperately for a reply from Lesley. I was so sure it would arrive with each post.

Eventually I wrote a nasty letter denouncing her irregular correspondence. Even the word 'bitch' was included. Her letter would inevitably arrive the following day.

I didn't ever receive a reply.

The months rolled on. I bought a camera and had a photographic tour of the area behind the base where there were the remnants of orchards originally planted and run by Italian colonists as part of Mussolini's empire. Now they were scrappy bits of addendum to Arab villages of corrugated iron shacks and half-clad children. Beyond the village were heaps of sand.

And a soccer season where I played left-half for the DSS on a sandy pitch with lines marked out in oil.

We also had a war.

Chapter Ten. War and 'de-mob'

King Farouk got the boot and Colonel Nasser took over control of Egypt. He nationalized the Suez Canal which saved the long haul around Cape Horn, but demanded transit taxes. When users refused payment, Nasser filled the canal with sunken shipping. This resulted, in part, in Great Britain, France and Israel declaring war on Egypt in 1956. In relatively close proximity, RAF Idris was an important base and troops sent from the UK arrived on their way to teaching Egypt not to meddle with trade routes.

Great excitement greeted the announcement of war. It was an exciting time. The powers that be on base issued us all with rifles, just why wasn't actually explained, and in the evening the Naafi was full of young men roaring out the old army songs – Tipperary, Siegfried Line (for God's sake), Lily Marlene. I shudder with embarrassment at the memory. The rifles were stacked up against a large stand, the beer flowed. We were ready to fight, by God we were! No- one questioned the right to go to war. Apart from anything else, it was the most heart-stirring event in our young lives.

They took the rifles away from us the following day. Someone had imagined an intruder and a shot had been fired. Hearing a shot, someone panicked and let rip with five rounds.

Fortunately no-one was hurt. The officers, one of whom had been seen wearing his gun- holster around his hips ready for a quick draw, also had their weapons withdrawn.

All the Arab dhobie and cleaning staff were shunted off base and spent the next six weeks lamenting bitterly just outside the wire. Each section had to provide men for sentry duty and on one of these I came horribly close to shooting a sergeant.

To some extent it was his own fault. Two of us were walking along the inside of the wire fence marking the boundary to the base. Lights periodically streamed upon us. Why they should have illuminated us rather than the darkness outside the fence was never explained. The guys we had relieved told us the sergeant who was in charge of the guard periodically showed up to test our alertness. When he showed himself from behind a tree I not only cried out the classic phrase, 'Halt who goes there?' but added to its authority by sliding the bolt and putting a bullet in the firing chamber.

The sergeant stopped. 'Careful with that, Carter,' he said.

'Okay, sarge,' I replied, 'I'll take it out.' Whereupon I opened the breech, removed the bullet and then closed the breech.

'Don't touch anything,' screamed the sergeant. He dropped down to the ground.

'Why not, Sarge. There's no bullet. Look.' I held it up.

He didn't actually call me an idiot, his expression was more forceful than that. I'd forgotten that when I closed the breech, the next bullet in the magazine would move up to take the place of the one I'd removed.

'Just put it down.'

Once I'd carefully placed the rifle on the ground the sergeant climbed to his feet, made the rifle safe, took a deep breath and walked away.

An understanding gentleman; we were amateur National Servicemen who'd done a week's course on rifles almost a year previously and then been handed something inherently lethal without any reminders. It truly was a wonder no-one died.

The US, who also had a base – Wheelus Field, some miles from us - stepped into the war, told the combatants to grow up and things returned to normal. The Arabs poured back on to the Base relieved at the return of employment, Nasser allowed Britain and France to clear out the ships he'd sunk, the British prime minister resigned, and I possessed a mouth-organ I'd bought from one of the soldiers who stopped overnight on base. It was my first musical instrument.

Now I was the only one left of the original four who'd shared the room I'd called home for well over a year. The one I'd been closest to was Don, an electrician. There was a small café which sold alcohol close to the base and we'd cycle there, me on the crossbar. Don would sink over ten beers while I sipped my drambuie or Tom Collins. I commented on this.

'The way to drink beer, Mike,' he answered, 'is slow. You won't get drunk if you just sit quietly, sip your glass, have a chat and eat something. I've drunk twelve pints at the local like that.'

Then we'd ride back to base laughing uproariously as the bike wobbled and we fell off into a ditch.

I remember seeing him off from the civil air terminus at Idris. People came and went. Soon it would be my turn.

Demobilisation came sooner than I thought it was as the Education Officer decided I should get early release to allow me to start the university year beginning in Sept 1958.

So back the way I'd come, shedding cutlery, checking in uniforms, and being fined for losing socks. And then into civvies and seeing my parents and brother and Sally, who'd just had twelve pups and was delighted to see me. And Lesley whom I'd rung and apologised to who brought over a book on Rome as a twenty-first birthday present. Hell, I was twenty-one.

Chapter Eleven. University years

After a week in the UK I succumbed to a bout of a sweating fever involving high temperatures, soaking wet sheets and an awful weakness. It reoccurred every two or three years or so for decades. Someone put it down to a malarial origin. It still occasionally pops up but my system copes better than that first time which delayed my arrival at Sheffield University for two weeks.

The delay meant that I missed out on soccer trials and didn't discover I should have enrolled for the honours course in History until half-way through the year. Neither of these actually had any lasting effect. I'd decided my life-style would have equal amounts of work and play. Essentially I've stuck to this philosophy and body and mind seemed to have appreciated the balance.

Basic training in the RAF had seen me try out boxing as a sport. I met up with another conscript who'd actually boxed in a circus, taking on all-comers in three round contests. He was lithe, light and not much taller than I but boy! Could he move!

'Weave, duck, dodge and smack 'em.'

He said he'd never been knocked down which in the circus constituted a win. As a substitute for soccer, I joined the university boxing club, fighting in the featherweight class. I kept up my soccer skills after watching a game on a playing-field just close to where I had digs. One side was a player short and as I'd sensibly brought along a pair of boots just in case, I signed on and played for the Hillsborough Baptist church for the rest of 1957. One Saturday, after a match, we sat discussing our team. We discovered that not one of us was a member of the church even the Captain whose wife was the sister of someone who knew someone who was.

The pitches we played on were situated sometimes in bogs, generally on uncut grass and once alongside a lake where two balls were lost. On a foggy afternoon in December we were on a pitch situated on a hill-top so you couldn't see from one goal-line to the other. Balls would fly out of the mist unexpectedly.

And unless you washed under a cold-water tap or in a stream you always returned home muddy.

Talking of home, I'd decided not to try for a place in a hall-of-residence. Too much like the institution I'd just left. I found 69, Rockley Road, Hillsborough close to the Sheffield United Football ground. It was owned by Mr and Mrs Platts. They had a ten year daughter named Christine and although both her parents are now dead I still retain links through an annual Christmas card. The years I spent with the Platts family were happy ones. I stayed there for the whole period of my university life sharing the first year with an engineer send to study in Sheffield by Rolls Royce.

Mrs Platts from the first made it clear she wouldn't do our washing. The alternatives were finding a local laundromat. There wasn't one. The other likely option was to send our dirty linen home. We both decided on the latter, both mothers being agreeable.

Once a week brown-paper parcels would arrive in Sheffield with the cleansed articles. It would return with the used ones. With me this was literally true. To conserve paper and string I would carefully wrap my dirty washing in the brown paper of my mother's parcel, stick on the appropriate stamp and send it back. And she would do likewise. Eventually a crumpled, sometimes torn parcel tied together with failing string would cause my mother to renew the packaging. Once the Sheffield end post office almost refused it on the grounds that stamps would no longer adhere to the creased paper.

Jame's mother always enclosed a fresh sheet of brown paper for her son to wrap his washing in. I now come to the point of this story.

On one occasion, Jame's washing didn't arrive. A letter from his mother did. She'd been informed that a railway employee, told to convey the parcel to the opposite platform, had tossed it blithely across the lines; it had clipped the other platform and bounced back onto the main lines where a train ran over it.

Could this have happened to my parcel I pondered? No, of course not. My parcel was obviously not designed to be tossed around. It was a lesson, but of what I've only a hazy idea. Maybe, striving for perfection isn't always the way to approach the problems of life.

The sailing-club used a class called Merlin-rockets and operated on a large reservoir created by submersing a village nestled amongst surrounding hills. I joined the club but it was the end of season and I only managed a few outings before winter set in.

The captain of the club was Dave, a medical student in his final two years. The Boatswain- the second in command - was another Dave who'd finished his national Service the previous year. He'd ended up a sergeant in the army. Had I come straight from school I would have been in awe of both of them. The RAF had made huge dents in the inferiority complex my height and accent had inflicted on me. I had emerged much more self-assured.

Home for Christmas. Lesley and I got engaged and I bought a small diamond ring for her. We had intensive passion sessions which never boiled over into sex although it might have saved our relationship if it had. Me, I had this naïve respect for conventions. Having a girl-friend was the right thing to do at this stage in life but what to do with her? My folks never told me. Certainly books did, the mates I'd shared billets with seemed to know. Lesley and I muddled along.

Sally had a new lease of life. We had the holidays, the Christmas vacations, Easter, and the summer together, but she was definitely older. She shared the second bedroom in the flat with Derek and me.

My brother had a unique way of stopping my snores. He kept a wet flannel alongside his bed and would hurl it at my face whenever necessary. Towards the end, Sally became another night-time disturbance, unable to last the whole night without relieving herself. This involved a trip with her and whom so ever she awoke, down the stairs and onto the lawn, carrying small shovel just in case.

Derek relates the occasion he staggered down the stairs and after five minutes discovered he'd lost the dog. He said he searched for ages before giving up and returning to find Sally curled up on his bed.

Eventually, during my last Easter Vacation from Sheffield, Sally developed rheumatism and would squeal in pain whatever the Vet prescribed. Dad eventually took her for a final visit.

We all cried. She'd been a family member for thirteen years. Unlike your children who grow away from you as the years pass, dogs grow closer. I can measure my life by the dogs I've loved, and cried over. Sally was the first. I was too young to feel close to Sandy.

I've photographs of both Lesley and Di with Sally.

My engagement to Lesley didn't stand up to the enforced separations of time and distance or, more probably, the fact that Di had entered my life. She was a year ahead of me. I was about seven months older.

It happened over a period of a term and I discovered later that she'd actually made enquiries and joined the Sailing Club since I ticked various boxes. We became an item as Lesley and I slid out of our engagement into a limbo relationship which juddered along during vacations.

Di and I sailed together. I tipped her in a couple of times and she laughed. We climbed into the sailing loft and had major snogging sessions. We danced together at the Union hops. She introduced me to facets of student life I hadn't experienced such as Chinese meals after a film, life in the hall and then life in her student flat. We once cycled from her house in Birmingham to Sheffield.

On her last summer vacation she went to Greece. It was in one of the periods when Lesley and I had somehow almost given up on each other, but not completely. She'd retained the engagement ring but wasn't wearing it. Maybe she suspected my double life.

'Okay,' I told myself. 'This isn't fair on either girl. But whom do I want?'

So I decided that I would visit Lesley in two days' time. If a letter arrived from Di in that time I would tell Lesley about Di. If it didn't I would ask Lesley to renew our vows to each other.

The letter arrived from Greece the following morning.

Lesley returned the ring and I never saw or spoke to her again although I can honestly say that there're not many days when I haven't thought about her. I hope she's had a happy life, and in absentia I've asked her to forgive me.

I know I could call myself stupid and maudlin. We'd probably never had had a successful marriage or had such super kids as Rob and Sally. Still, at the back of my mind, there's a feeling of guilt about the whole situation.

Before I leave this period of my life I should mention Fred. During the university vacations I worked for the Lewisham Borough Council mowing lawns. The official hours were from 7.30 am until 5 pm and with an hour for lunch and two quarters of an hour as morning and afternoon smokos, this entailed an eight hour day. Fred interpreted the day's structure differently. 'See you at about eight, Mike.'

A council truck would deliver the necessary equipment – a couple of hand-push lawnmowers, rakes, slashers and Fred (he always got the driver to pick him up). He'd arrive about eight when we'd immediately pop round to the nearest café for a cuppa or, if it was too far for Fred, who was seventy- three, bring out our vacuum flasks. We'd discuss the groundwork of the day before breaking off for the scheduled 10 o'clock smoko. With a café close this would last an hour and involve Fred's commentary on local and international news as presented by the Daily Mirror. Serious work began about eleven before we knocked off at twelve for lunch.

Fred, treating this period as an opportunity for a nap, rarely reappeared before two. Depending on the weather, 'we're not paid to get soaked,' if it rained and 'sod this for a lark, let's find some shade,' if the sun shone, we'd get stuck into the lawns around various council buildings until 3.pm. After a half hour's tea-break, we'd return to clear oddments before the truck arrived at 4.30 to return us to the depot.

The only occasion we actually worked solidly until 4.30, the truck for some reason having failed to turn up, Fred put in for an hour's overtime.

Another job I found was with the IRD. It involved finding files. I acted as support for Harold, a portly gentleman who suffered from vertigo meaning I had to fetch him any file that required a ladder to bring it within reach. No computers in those days, just miles of shelving ten feet high. Where was I? Yes, at university, of course.

I once cycled from Sheffield to London. It took 17 hours on a push-bike with three gears, but only the top one worked. Geez, I was fit in those days. A year or two later and presumably that much wiser I bought myself a motor-bike, a 250cc Velocette of 1936 vintage. I named her Eliza Jane. She did make my progress around the country easier.

The Daves left University. Rod became Captain and I became Boatswain of the Sailing club; I gained a half-blue in my second year and a full blue in the last. I played for the University third eleven at soccer and was picked for the second when another period of the malarial sweat hit me and the doctors decreed no major exercise. So soccer went down the drain. Boxing had been given up in my first year. I had three fights and lost them all.

Fighting as a featherweight at 9 stone 2 pounds meant I came up against opponents taller and with a longer reach. They danced around jabbing a fist in my face and I just couldn't get close. Of course I also lacked the skill. I managed to reach the final of a northern University completion. There were only three of us in the featherweight division, I won a place in the final by drawing the right card. The other two fought a vicious and exciting bout to decide who would meet me in the final.

Whoever did, disposed of me in two rounds when the referee stopped the fight on humanitarian grounds.

Sheffield University actually ended up winning the competition. It helped that I was runner-up in the featherweight class.

After the University competition, the Boxing-club captain and I had a conversation and he talked of the detrimental effects of being pounded on the head. I found myself agreeing. I was playing soccer and sailing, so the physical side of life was being attended to.

I also had a chat with Sarge the manager and trainer of the boxing club and said I thought the ring wasn't my forte. He didn't try to dissuade me.

Sarge was, I discovered later, responsible for allocating the sports budget of the university. The sailing club had more funds allocated to it the year I was Boatswain than ever before. Not really a co-incidence. We even bought a new boat.

Di graduated and found a job in Harwell working on developing a standard human being so that effects of radiation on the non-standard could be gauged. I finished another year at Sheffield graduating with a BA Honours second class first level (there were two) in History.

The night when the results were read out we were treated to a meal at the prof's house. I'd got on well with him. He'd allowed me to do the Hons course even though I'd missed out half a year's lectures on the understanding that I'd catch up on the work missed. The subject that year was 19th century Europe. I'd enjoyed this period and studied it in depth at O and A level. I'd dug out my notes and found them adequate for the honours course with a minimum of decoration.

I'd written various essays on arcane subjects trying to inject a sociological element. On one occasion when I'd had two Roman subjects discussing philosophy while peeling an enormous pile of potatoes (a task I understood) he'd gently pointed out that spuds weren't current in Europe until Raleigh had brought them back from America. That was during the Tudors period.

None of our year got as low as a BA level 4 which was a fail but a number received a 3 which wasn't really adequate, even for teaching. One of the guys complained bitterly that those receiving the higher grades hadn't benefited from the full flavor of university life. When I asked him to explain the remark he spoke of parties and drinks and smokes. I commiserated but fundamentally my view was that I'd come to University to obtain a degree which would supply me with the necessary qualifications to get a decent job. Fun was a bonus. Tough titty.

One of the girls gained a First Class degree.

My parents came to the graduation ceremony. I returned to the flat, now without a dog at weekends, decided that I wouldn't bother with training college and would teach at Charlton Secondary Modern School for boys, where the Deputy Principal, a George Carter, not a relative, persuaded me to become a probationary assistant, learning the art of teaching under the mentorship of himself. I'd already taught there for a few weeks during the long vacations when a student, filling in where needed. I knew the boys, I knew the staff. George said he'd see my classes were the easy ones. And at the end of the year someone from the Education Department would inspect me and provide a certificate recognizing me as a teacher.

On top of it all, instead of being a student for another year, I'd be earning money.

So I signed up for Charlton and spent the next two years there. I honestly think neither I or the future generations I was to teach suffered for my lack of formal teaching instruction. There are, I reckon, two basic requirements. Firstly know your subject. Secondly, know how to entertain.

Chapter Twelve. Marriage; and Charlton Secondary School for Boys.

Possibly through a distrust of leaving to me to my own devices in London, Di joined me at Charlton later on that year. She resigned from Harwell, moved in with a couple in a flat close by and entered the teaching profession on the same terms as I had – picking it up as we went along under the benevolent eyes of some senior members of staff.

Major Ford was principal, always addressed as 'Sir' by boys and staff alike. There were three women teachers, one young, recently married, one the wife of Joe Moss, a man who could reduce a class of fourteen year old thugs to quivering jelly by merely slitting his eyes. On one occasion, after it became known that Di and I were headed for New Zealand, he made half the school watch an entire film run backwards explaining that this is what we would encounter on the other side of the world.

It was a rainy day, sports had been cancelled and three classes had been combined. I watched these tough kids sit quietly through the whole session. Unbelievable. Joe was the man who's idea of Phys. Ed. in summer was to sit under a tree and throw tennis balls for the children to chase. The one who collected the most had the task of throwing the next lot of balls.

Other members of staff included Bill Williams who advocated refereeing soccer games from the pavilion if it was inclement outside, and George Carter, who was once approached by a crowd of fourth formers who had decided Rugby was more suited to their baser instincts. George said he would train them.

'Sorry it's a soccer ball, but I'm not buying a thing that doesn't bounce right until I'm sure you're keen. Okay, start jogging around the field tossing the ball to each other. When I blow the whistle the nearest boys to the one with the ball, jump on him and throw him to the ground and rip the ball away, Then you carry on. Do this until you're told to stop.'

Ten minutes of this and Rugby was a dead duck at Charlton.

Alan Weir was the Science teacher and an old Roan similar to me and George. He was irritated by the fact that neither I, nor Di who, joined me on the staff after resigning from Harwell, had undertaken a post-graduate teaching diploma. However he took Di under his wing and we both completed our probationary year at Charlton and at the end of the following school year were sufficiently well-trained to be acceptable to the New Zealand Educational recruiting officers.

The music teacher was another member of staff who had a lasting influence on me. He had persuaded the authorities to provide the school with a heap of brass instruments. His enthusiasm and drive meant Charlton, for all its tough, dockside face could put up a band of over fifty boys. They would all blast forth at morning assembly with the national anthem and a hymn. Admittedly thirty of these were recorder players from whose ranks the brass players of the future were chosen, but the resulting cacophony appealed to the spirits of most boys with a sometimes unmusical competition between vocalists and players.

Two fourth formers confronted Di and me shortly after our arrival.

Boy One: What d'you play, Sir?

Me: Er... I've a mouth organ.

Boy One: You any good?

Me: No.

Boy Two: (To Di). D'you play anything, Miss?

Di: I learnt the piano.

Boy One: Well you both oughta learn the recorder.

So we took lessons from them.

The recorder is an under-rated instrument. I've played it in an Irish Band, taught it up to Trinity Grade Two at Onewhero, heroically performed in front of a pub crowd each week at an open mic night, tootled along with a geriatric band of ukulele players and had someone ask me if it was a special sort of flute. To most listeners the recorder is something they left in Form two (as it was once called) but played with a bit of feeling, a bit, not heaps, of practice and especially if augmented by a guitar and with an amp's reverb turned up full, boy, it can sound good.

Thank you Charlton.

On August 12th 1961 Di and I were married by an enormous size minister in Birmingham and following a reception, set off for our honeymoon and holiday at a hotel in Cornwell. Di's parents had persuaded to go there, they'd spent the first days of their own married life many years sago.

On reflection we should have packed our belongings onto the back of Eliza Jane and just toured around. The hotel ambience was all wrong. We felt more in common with the students who formed the backbone of the domestic staff than with the other guests. Ultimately we hired a couple of push bikes and explored the by-ways, occasionally trying out the ice cold waters on small surf-boards and then swigging cups of hot chocolate to get rid of the blue colour in my extremities.

As with many holidays demanding special attention I wrote a log of events. Including as it did some of the marital experiments. I have since removed several unnecessarily graphic descriptions but the log of our Cornwall enterprise still exists as a chopped up account of what not to do on a honeymoon.

On the way home Di was stung by a bee which disappeared down the front of her blouse. Half of me disbelieved in its existence and it joined the saga of unsuccessful beginnings.

Our marriage lasted just under fifty years, much to the surprise of Di's parents and our children. I attempted to answer the question of how we'd stayed together at her funeral in 2010. I said that we'd made a commitment. Our marriage lasted because we wanted it to last. Life together, its memories, its successes, its strivings, its laughter and tears was better than life apart.

She helped me in what I attempted, never tried to hold me back. I hope I gave her similar support and a solid base of mutual trust.

We returned to Charlton a married couple and occupied two rooms in a large house in Blackheath for three pounds a week. Each morning we journeyed to school, Di on the back of Eliza Jane clutching a couple of bags. The motorbike wasn't the easiest to start, and as this involved heaving up and down on the kick-starter I often arrived at school a nasty smelly, sweaty heap under all the top layers of motor-cycle clothing.

Eliza Jane merits a couple of paragraphs. She cost me $40, had grid front forks and a large flywheel mounted outside the one cylinder 250cc engine. I knew very little about engines, on one occasion dismantling bits of the carburetor and carefully making a template for a gasket, drawing around the outside of the intake but omitting to remove the interior cardboard which, once I had triumphantly replaced everything, unsurprisingly prevented any traffic of mixture to the engine. If you don't understand any of this then that's how I felt after fighting the engine for hours before light dawned.

Most technology mystifies me. I cope by animating it, giving it character and personality. Our vehicles have always been named. We've had in succession Pug, Archie, Rommel, Monty, Newton, Bubbles and now Lily.

Boats obviously are female, and variously called 'Ronaki' although I have a sneaking suspicion the frostbite made it essentially male, 'Here'n There' which was a heron-class dinghy and so named by its builder. There have been Monty Mason, 'Blossom', 'Tess' and Simone, all of whom help towards this story.

It's remiss of me to forget Charley whom I bought a couple of years ago and who now, in 2018, sails in the in the Tauranga harbour

I have yet to name a computer but I do believe they respond to feelings. And yes, you'll say it's me being psychotic. Well, if it helps me, great! Let me admit to my psychosis.

Eliza Jane and I joined with Alan Musset in a trip around Scotland, he roaring ahead on his BSA 300; another time, with Di on the back, the chain fell off while circumnavigating Trafalgar Square. A traffic cop stopped by one of the lions and guarded me as I fixed the chain.

One of the bike's idiosyncracies was having the battery dribble away overnight. This was solved by putting a switch between battery and engine. Twice while at school the battery was fully discharged by the end of the day, necessitating lots of boys shoving me around the playground to jump start it. Investigation disclosed that a group of fourth-formers had been joyriding around the playground. I caught one of them and conscious of the fact that they were all bigger, tougher and less moral they I, said, somewhat weakly: 'You're not supposed to ride around in teacher's cars…or on their motorbikes but for heaven's sake, if you do, just turn that switch off by the battery or it's bloody hard to start.'

We left it at that. The D.P ultimately found someone doing the playground circuit during a Social

Study lesson and despite the kid pleading that 'Mr Carter said we could,' Eliza Jane was given a lockable shed for the rest of my stay at Charlton.

To finish tales of this era, one of my favourite memories of Charlton also occurred after I'd given a colourful account of the battle of Trafalgar. One of the most forgettable was a 12 year old vomiting after I'd related a gruesome historic incident involving a red hot poker.

We'd found an advertisement in the Times Educational Gazette asking for applications from teachers to bring light and culture to New Zealand.

Di's science degree impressed the appointment board and as she wouldn't go without me I was bundled in as an extra who could do things like History and Geography.

Di had a rough introduction.

'Any questions?' she asked the new class expectantly.

A hand shot up.

'Yes?'

'Did you know you've got a hair growing out the middle of your forehead?'

Di broke a stick over a cheeky eleven year old's backside and the kid's father, a large muscular guy in overalls came up to complain. Di was hauled into the DP's office to meet him.

The dockworker looked down at Di. 'You wopped him?' he asked incredulously.

'Yes,' answered Di. 'He was rude. Very.'

'Good. Do it anytime.' And the concerned father shook Di's hand and walked out.

That was Charlton. Neither Di nor I had any official teacher training but the two years at Charlton gave us insights into the human side of teaching. And this is infinitely more important than academic brilliance. As a teacher you have this audience of about thirty. You have to amuse them, entertain, cheer them when they've got something right and spend time when they've got it wrong. You compete with television, bloody old Facebook, sodding twitter and instan-stuffing-gram. Get on that stage and give 'em hell.

I wonder how many teacher training colleges give that sort of advice.

We had a great send-off. As they'd given us wedding presents less than a year previously I asked for large signed card. I still have it.

After much debate we and both sets of parents bought the latest in communication technology – tape recorders. Then, without much in the way of farewells Di and I climbed on a DC6 at Heathrow and set off on a nine day trip to New Zealand.

Chapter Thirteen. New Zealand

Because the crew flying the plane did the whole journey without changing, we stopped periodically so they could catch up on their nerves. We stopped at various Air US Bases and had days off in New York, where we gazed open-mouthed at the patches of blue sky between the skyscrapers and San Francisco where we were served by bunny-rabbit hostesses as intrigued with our accents as we were by their uniforms. At Hawaii despite my confidence in being able to master the art of surfing in deep waters, I was ignominiously ordered ashore by a life-guard.

We learnt to have eggs either East-west or sunny side up, a concoction initially beyond comprehension, and descended dazedly from the plane at Whenuapai to be bussed into Auckland and fed at a Temperance hotel where we met Fred Woods the deputy Assistant of Onewhero District High School. We'd chosen this when presented with a choice of positions. It was only fifteen miles from the sea and a large wide river offered the possibilities of inland sailing.

The following morning a train took us to Tuakau and we waited somewhat subdued outside the local pub which still had a rail outside to which we expected to see horses attached. Thence a taxi transported us across the Tuakau Bridge and up Punt Hill to Onewhero.

As we crossed the Waikato, seeing islands on either side of the bridge and the wide, slow-moving river disappearing into a misty distance, our spirits lifted. This was going to be home for the three years we had contracted for. It was now starting to look good. And throughout the decades which have raced past, that trip over the Waikato still makes the heart beat gratefully. The river is a moat which keeps at bay things I fear – and I'm not going to list them. It's my moat and I'm grateful for it.

Now, in 2018, living near Mount Maunganui I realise I'm still fortunate to be hunkered down behind geographical barriers – before me stretches the Tasman, behind, the Kaimai Range. Maybe we all need some psychological comfort blanket to feel secure. Security's important. The pre-war years, the constant fear during the war and the austerity that followed made security the major ambition of my parents' generation and I'm sure it's rubbed off on me.

The road from Tuakau Bridge wound its way through undulating hillsides until Di and I arrived at the school-bus bay and curious eyes watched us from the standard four class-room and the long building beside it. A short tubby man emerged from the latter.

'Guess you're the new teachers. Welcome to Onewhero District High School. I'm Graham Bale; I teach woodwork.'

By this time the lady from the classroom had arrived with a small girl. 'Good to see you. Mavis Hatwell. This is Joan; she'll take you down to see the principal.'

Whither we were conducted, passing a swimming pool, a large house and a huge pile of coal. We knocked on a door.

'Mike and Di Carter, eh? Good to see you. Long journey out and feeling tired?' The headmaster was shortish and slim. He quickly disabused us of any need for formality, dismissing my hesitant, 'Good morning, Sir,' with a laugh.

'The name's Laurie. I'll show you around the place and then we'll have a chat and I think the DP is putting you up until you find a place of your own.'

We were swept into and out of various classrooms. The general verdict, I discovered later, was that a couple of midgets had been unloaded on them. But judgement would be reserved until they'd seen us perform.

Fred Woods, the senior secondary assistant took us in for the first month. He lived in one of the four staff-houses the school possessed. I'd best explain the school hierarchy. The top person was the principal who was usually a trained primary teacher. Beneath him were the senior assistants. Fred was responsible for the senior school, students in forms 3, 4, 5, 6 or in modern terms, years 9, 10, 11 and 12. He taught English and had a number of teachers in the secondary department teaching Maths, Social Studies, History, Geography, various sciences and technical subjects.

The middle, school forms 1 and 2 was led by Matt Tawhiri. He was the first Maori we'd met. He was a consummate musician and apart from looking after the middle school taught music to the seniors. One of the strengths of the District School set-up was the ability to switch teachers between the various age groups.

Matt told us, almost off-handedly, that he wasn't allowed upstairs in the Pukekohe cinema.

'Maoris aren't allowed in the circle,' he explained.

I couldn't believe it. Thank God things have changed. I was all for setting the place on fire but I guess that wouldn't have helped.

The Junior School was given over to the infants through to the standards 3,4,5,6, and the principal kept a benign eye on these. The technical department included woodwork, needle-work and cooking facilities. These were shared not only by the Onewhero Middle school but also by surrounding primary schools, in this case, Pukekawa,
Te Kohanga and Glen Murray, whose students came by bus once a week.

Pupils in the secondary department would include pupils from these latter schools whose parents had opted not to send them off to boarding schools.

When Di and I arrived there was a different house system for the Junior School and the Secondary Department. I became a member of Huia, the others being Kiwi, Tui and (I think) Kaka. This house system and nomenclature changed about five times over the next fifty years.

The origin of the Motto 'One for all, all for one,' is disputed. Some of the older inhabitants say it refers to the primary schools which sent their pupils to the

Onewhero District High School for their secondary education; others maintain that the 'all' was the various departments within the school: Infant, Junior and Secondary. I veer to the former explanation. There are two lines on the school crest with stars on either side of them. I think the two lines represent the Waikato River and the stars the contributing schools.

We started the day after our arrival. Di took over Chemistry and Biology at Form Six level plus General Science in the lower classes. She hated Physics and Maths which messed up the calculations of the principal who, unsure what a degree in Physiology entailed, had penciled in Di as a Maths teacher. Consequently, I took up her Maths classes, History at Form 5 and 6 level and odds and ends of Social Studies.

We'd arrived.

Onewhero. Translated this means 'red earth'. It was the centre of a rural area of about two hundred families. In 1962, well before the Labour party chopped out subsidized farming and the UK still accepted everything NZ could produce, the farmers were tops. Not that they flaunted their wealth. They worked alongside their workers. Unless prompted by their wives they wore shorts, gumboots an old tee-shirt and some form of headgear most of the time. Saturdays saw workers and farmers turn out for the local rugby fifteen, slipping slowly from the first fifteen to the reserves, the golden oldies and finally the sideline with drunken revels following the game. But the following morning they'd all be up before dawn milking the cows.

In summer there might be tennis, many farmers owning their own grass court, or surfing down at Port Waikato. Kids might be taken by their mothers to the small pool in the school grounds. Or the boat would be hooked onto the back of the ute and driven over the bar for fishing. But always, there was the afternoon and dawn milkings; except during the wet cold months of June when the cows were dried off and there was a chance of long sleep-ins and maybe a holiday to Fiji.

The children of farmers and workers all attended the local primary school staffed by teachers drafted in to do their 'country service'. It was an equalitarian society where teachers learnt about rural life and often married into it. The only blip in this equality was the departure of most farmers' children to boarding school for their secondary education but by this time Jack knew he was as good as his master and the ones who went to the local country school weren't any worse off academically. In fact it was the daily distance kids would have to travel to and from school. In some instances an hour either way over gravel roads that really was a major factor. Most of the boys would return to the farm. Some of the girls returned with a husband who'd take over the farm. The structure of the district hasn't really changed all that much in half a century.

And there was the district dental nurses with their own set-up. They usually ended up marrying some local farmer and stayed in the district.

After a few weeks with Fred, our box from England arrived and we were offered a house in the Kaipo

Flats for two pounds a week. The Flats is, geographically, a caldera, one of the largest in the southern hemisphere. It is a volcano which collapsed in on itself leaving a rim of hills like a mighty arena looking down on a circular area of flat pasture land. In 1962 this supported eight family-farms - Nelson Pellow, Lobb, Mitchell, Costar, Chris Pellow, Bovill, Halford, van Vught. Now it's been reduced to five - Mitchells, Costars, Pellows, Bovills and van Vughts. A small but successful cheese-making enterprise now exists in one segment of the Flats. 'Mercer Cheese' has won many medals for its produce sold from a small shop close to the Waikato River.

The house we rented nestled under the rim of the caldera, two paddocks back from a gravel road. For the few days it took to assemble our motor-bike and side-car, we caught the school bus to school, picked up at the farm-gate. It was gradually filled by more children as it journeyed around the Flats. Nowadays apart from one stretch of gravel, the Kaipo Flats is blessed with tar-sealed roads. Gravel was a vast improvement to some of the back-country farm roads composed of clay and almost impassable in winter.

Under the eyes of eleven year old David and Mike, the twin sons of Kath and Nelson Bovill from whom we were renting the house, I attached the side-car to the BSA 500cc m/ bike we had bought in England and posted over to NZ. It had been a nasty decision leaving Eliza Jane behind but we'd been assured many times that some form of vehicle was essential and a two-wheeled one unsafe on the country roads. We'd compromised by donating the Velocette to Charlton and purchasing Pug, so named from the PGU English number plate.

Although common in the UK a motor-bike combination was rare in New Zealand and completely unknown in Onewhero. The boys stopped digging the holes for the main posts of the fence being constructed around the house and watched agog as I finally added fuel to the petrol tank and then jumped on the kick-start.

There was a sudden roar and to everyone's astonishment the whole thing burst into flames.

'Water,' I yelled. The boys ran to an outside tap, I grabbed a rag and wrapped it round the flames. The fire – a leaking fuel line combined with a magneto spark - was extinguished. The boys regarded me with awe and, not exactly admiration, but as something essentially peculiar.

Even now, when I make a return trip to Onewhero, people speak nostalgically of the motor-cycle combination that really nailed our reputation as eccentric limeys. Over the next three years this changed to a deep and reciprocated love.

Chapter Fourteen. 1962 – 1967 The first visit

These years were intended to be a working holiday. Instead they were a period which not only consolidated our value-system but introduced us to an environment where those values could expand in so many different directions.

Firstly there was village life. You couldn't hide from people. They cared. There was the manual telephone exchange, 'Mike's just gone past, Di. Should be home soon.' And the shared line. 'Sorry to butt in but I couldn't help hearing that...' The announcement from an infant delivering its morning report, 'Well, Daddy said to Mummy that... '; the gossip at the women's local branch of federated farmers. There were also chats over beer at the after-match functions, although to be honest these were usually conducted in incomprehensible grunts.

People matter in a village. If there's an accident, there's always offers of help, or cakes, or replacement furniture. I guess in crowded cities we don't own much space so we hide in the bit we do have.

When we turned up at the village hall the first time for Friday night's movie, we found a packed house. The audience put out the chairs stored in the supper room, Graham Bale's son, seated in a little room near the ceiling, threaded a reel of film into the projector. The librarian told everyone she was closing the library and locked the doors guarding the shelves of books. And the show began.

The film, it evolved was only part of the show. At its conclusion the whole audience poured outside to line the pavement. They watched as Di and I put on our jackets. Di lifted the lid and climbed into the sidecar. I clicked the lid shut, mounted onto the machine, held my breath and kicked the starter.

And then we puttered off, everyone waving like mad. I think there was an air of disappointment that nothing dramatic had happened; but I could see some clapping.

School was also a different world. For a start there were girls as well as boys. No pupil was addressed by his or her surname. We were rarely addressed as 'Sir' or 'Miss'. It was Mr or Mrs Carter.

Laurie, the principal, had told us that one of his important jobs was to oversee the welfare of his staff. He had a party at his house every Friday where Matt Tawhari played the piano and we gathered around singing, drinking beer and eating whatever had been brought along.

'Bring a plate.' It took us an embarrassing moment the first we obeyed that request. 'It means, of course, a plate containing something. It is not indicative of a shortage of plates.

There was Chris who taught English and French. He'd arrived from the UK the previous year. Tony taught art and Neil taught Geography, Ivor taught Science and

Jenny Begg was the Maths teacher. Most of the staff turned up but the Friday get together was designed essentially for the single who would otherwise have a lonely evening. Tuakau was the nearest pub, but not, in those days, the most salubrious. Pukekohe was too far. Matt Tawhari banged out old favourites on the piano. Laurie looked after his troops and in the process had a happy bunch of teachers.

The village was fortunate that pioneers had seen to the establishment of a recreational reserve. There were two rugby fields, a pavilion funded by the rugby club, a large paddock used for grazing stock, and a couple of tennis courts. In summer a wicket was banged into shape in the middle of the main rugby pitch. Major agricultural events were held there where pet calves, lambs, and chickens were shown. This livestock was expanded over the years and came to include dogs and goats and anything that could be considered alive. Come to think of it, once this included stones.

The first Christmas we were in Onewhero, the rugby club held an athletic day with events for all age groups. There were three-legged races for kids and adults, ditto for ordinary running races. A handicapper distributed benefits to various competitors by casual scrutiny. By virtue of my size I was given a twenty yard lead over the rest of the field in the 100 yard dash. Wearing my spiked running shoes, a relative innovation in Onewhero, I won easily. I entered the 220 race without any concessions being made to age or height and won that too. It helped my image considerably.

Digressing slightly, my speed on the track brought me to the attention of the rugby committee and later the following year, it was suggested I join the football club. I joined the club enthusiastically despite never having actually ever seen a rugby match let alone played in one, after all it couldn't be all that difficult. Just catch a ball, run with it and kick it as far as you could.

I was disabused of these concepts very quickly and ended up playing on the wing for the under 21 year old side despite being 24. I was given special dispensations for ignorance, size and general ineptitude.

In that first season I eventually ended up positioned hopefully and comparatively uselessly, on the wing. At our level if the ball got passed from hand to hand someone would drop it before it reached me or the centre would make a strategic kick. A screaming mob of forwards, uncannily following the pattern of play George demanded of the fourth form at Charlton, would then converge on the ball and the unfortunate person waiting to catch it, until a whistle blew and a more organized brawl- called a scrum – would ensue. Occasionally the opposing wing would receive the ball and sprint in my direction. Browny Taupo, a short solid Maori who played at half-back told me his philosophy. 'Run at them, Mike, and go for their legs. Keep your head out of the way and smash in. Don't worry about them passing the ball before you reach them.'

I lasted the one season as a novice before discovering Pukekohe had a soccer club which I joined with alacrity. Ten years or so later together with Dave Bovill and his younger brother Pete, I had another season playing rugby for the Onewhero 2nd Fifteen and managed to score a try. Great stuff!

Incidentally, our team possessed an exceptionally good half back. I remember vividly the occasion he failed to turn up for a match leaving the message that his wife was playing netball and he had to look after the family. Was he ahead of his time! More likely his wife was. Suffice to say, village life was pretty full.

Pretty obviously school played a major role in our lives. Our relationship with students, staff and parents was great. No-one tired of our accents – mine cockney, Di's Brum - so lessons were listened to attentively, at least for the first few months by which time the content also registered. We made friends with a number of parents and were invited to evening meals and afternoon teas where the kids would sit goggle-eyed as they listened to our often hyperbolic accounts of teaching at Charlton and life in general in the homeland. And in that first visit to New Zealand it was obvious that England was 'Home,' even if the speaker had been born in Onewhero.

New friends included the O'Briens. Jim gave Di a cow's hide to cure; it's still on a floor. Jim and Koa had four children, two boys, two girls and we taught them all. John and Flora Halford were our neighbours to the south of us. Flora was a Scotswoman who'd married John after he'd been repatriated to England following the debacle of Crete in 1943(?).

She disliked most of the Onewhero women suspecting they resented a foreigner marrying one of their own. John and Flora had two boys and a girl; Bob, Johnny and Marion. Kath and Nelson, our landlords, lived about four paddocks to our north. There were three boys and a girl, Dave, Mike, Pete and Cheryl. The other close family friends were the Maurenbrechers. These merit a paragraph to themselves.

Anton (Ton) Maurenbrecher was the epitome of the Lieutenant Colonel he'd been in the Dutch Army, tall, upright with a commanding presence. He was an engineer, owning skills in building and machinery making him a welcome asset to Onwhero. He and his wife had four children, three girls and a boy. Henny Maurenbrecher had borne four children during her previous marriage. They were with her when the Japanese invaded Indonesia and the two girls died in the concentration camp which had been set up to imprison the Dutch. Her husband had been killed in a tank. Ton accepted the two surviving sons as his own.

Henny's experiences in the concentration camp were of punishment, slow starvation and death. That she survived she credited to a faith that kept her strong and sane. It was something akin to Buddhism, but not really. Di and I taught all of Ton and Henny's children – Noes, Yet, Barbara and Tony and knew Pete and Hans, the surviving sons quite well.

Yet another strand to Onewhero living was/is the local drama club. This was an offshoot of the Women's branch of federated farmers which, requiring the occasional male in productions, branched out as an entity in its own right sometime in the 1940s.

Arriving in September, I was in time to appear in a one act play at Christmas entitled 'Irresistible Albert,' so-called because of Albert's ability to charm all classes of women. As Albert, I was ultimately tapped on the head by a doctor's receptionist thereby curing my problem. The girl playing the receptionist, contrary to the director's instructions, used a real mallet which caused a temporary black-out. It would, I suppose, have made a dramatic note on which to terminate this story. Tough, there's at least another fifty years to go. Aaaargh.

Over all my years, there was the wide range of animals we took on. Firstly, there were the goats Gruff and Hannah. One of the local farmers came across Gruff after it's mother had been shot dead, and we brought him up. Hannah turned up a week later as a companion, for the same reason. They became loving pets, cheap to feed, intelligent and house-trained.

The only drawback was their inability to distinguish what they were permitted to eat, from what they were not. There wasn't much of a garden, and they generally made short work of anything there was.

One of the boys at school arrived with a small joey and presented it to Di. The baby opossum also became a Carter. It would curl up on a shoulder, its prehensile tail coiled around a neck, lazily watching proceedings. Eventually Oswalda moved out of her basket into the roof, popping down at dusk to rattle the back door knob until one of us opened the door. Then she would eat the plate of raisins before climbing on the back of one of the goats and, in winter, sleep with them in front of the fire.

One night Di made an exceptionally alcoholic fondue, the remnants of which she gave to Ossie. That night a drunken opossum could be heard staggering around above our heads with an occasional thump as it lost its grip on a rafter.

Apart from the roof many of its daylight sojourns were spent atop the cistern above our loo, one of the old-fashioned devices with a chain. The language of the refined lady on whose head Ossie jumped reverted swiftly into vernacular more frequently heard at the rugby club. Extricating an opossum from the hair of the hysterical lady seated on a loo wasn't easy. Fortunately Di was there to help.

And to complete the menagerie I bought Di a horse named Trixie. She'd belonged to a family living in the corner of the Flats but she needed more attention than the kids there wanted to give. Di had switched to part-time teaching in the second year so she now had the time.

One of my favourite memories of Trixie is sitting on the sheep-skin, no saddle, behind Di on Trixie's back singing 'I'm Henry the Eighth I am' at the top of my voice'. And years later Kath Bovill asking me to sing it at her 70th birthday because she'd remembered my voice booming the chorus around the Flats.

Finally, these years re-kindled my passion for boats which had been born in Idris and blossomed for us both on the reservoirs of Sheffield.

New Zealand seas aren't much different.

Chapter Fifteen. Exploring New Zealand

The first Christmas in New Zealand saw us travelling northwards to Cape Reinga. It was a vastly different place from the crowded tourist destination Bernadette and I visited only last year.

On the earlier visit Di and I had left the tar- sealed road somewhere near Kaitaia and, trailing clouds of dust, eventually arrived at the light-house without seeing anyone else. A Maori guy we encountered on the road invited us onto his farm to see some caves.

We only ever received kindness from the Maori. They were hospitable, generous and helpful. From Cape Reinga we came south again and wound our way around the coast to Gisborne. The motor-bike sidecar combination fascinated everyone who saw it.

While up north we'd discovered the camp site at Te Kao was full, so we called in at a nearby farm and asked permission to put up our tent in one of their paddocks. We were still calling them 'fields'.

'Sure. The girls'll show you.' The big Maori farmer had a grin on his face. 'Youse from England?'

'Yes, I'm from London; the name's Mike. This is my wife, Di'

He introduced himself and his daughters. Then asked, 'Youse like it here, eh?' Everyone asked that question almost as if they wanted confirmation of what they believed but weren't sure about.

'Really beautiful.'

The two girls, aged eleven or twelve, took us down to the beach and watched us pitch a tent. Then they walked into the sea, groped around some rocks and came back with what resembled a couple of hedgehogs.

'Do you like kina?'

'Well, er...'

'It's good. Taste it.' With which one of them banged the hedge-hoggy thing on a rock. It broke open to reveal a white centre. I looked at the girl.

'You eat it.'

'Er; right. I'll get a spoon.'

I gathered later that spoons weren't really necessary. Kina is okay anywhere, anyhow.

Later that evening the girls reappeared with a crayfish for us. Thank goodness that was cooked

And on the following day with many thanks we returned to Onewhero via Te Kuiti where the local butcher tried to persuade us to change our allegiance and remain there. 'Lovely place, close to the ski-fields, east coast, west coast...'

Back in Onewhero we enquired further about Te Kuiti and came to the conclusion we'd chosen the better spot.

But we'd been to the Bay of Islands and lusted after the sparkling blue seas and the scattering of islands. We'd stood in the Waitangi grounds watching sails move magically across the white flecked waves.

'We must get a boat.'

Later, at the beginning of 1963 we bought Ronaki. She was a wooden, clinker built Frostbite - an open dinghy about twelve feet long with a gaff rig and no jib. With her we sealed ourselves into New Zealand. With her we explored the islands close to Kawakawa bay: Pakahi, Quarry and then Ponui.

Our best trip was when we took her to Thames and after sleeping overnight in the Thames Yacht Club sail-locker set off the following morning to Coromandel.

'Good luck and fair winds, Ronaki,' boomed a loud hailer as we set off.

It was us being Francis Chichester sailing around the world, and 'Seagulls and Amazons', rolled into one. And it is still after all these years. Everything is so vivid; the seas jollied along by the wind, the sun glinting on the waves, the salt air. We took it in turns to steer or to control the mainsheet. I was concerned with the open bow. If a wave broke over it there was nothing to stop the water just pouring in.

We stopped halfway up the coast at Te Puna where we camped. Then on to our destination, Coromandel harbour. The wind rose. I consulted the chart.

'Dead man's point and then we're into the harbour,' I muttered. 'Okay, stand by to jibe.' Then for some reason the tiller sipped from my grasp, the boom slammed across and Ronaki tipped on her side.

Di grabbed the tiller, we both leapt to windward and Ronaki, half-full of water came upright.

With pounding hearts we sailed gently down the harbour, the Manaia peninsular on our right and Rangipukea Island to port (to return to the nautical). A sheltered bay on the island beckoned and gratefully we turned into the still waters. Out of the wind we drifted to the sandy beach, hauled Ronaki out of reach of the tide, found a grassy bank and stretched out on it.

'Thanks, Di.'

We grinned at each other, felt the warmth of the sun wash away all the horrible 'might-have-beens'. Then a voice broke into the silence.

'Washed up?'

Kevin O' Halloran was an ex school-inspector who had bought a section on the island and shifted over the tools and materials in his yacht from his base on Waiheke to build a cottage there. He was well over seventy and his wife had died some years previously. Later we discovered there were two middle-aged single ladies living close to his Waiheke house who were vying for his attention.

After a day of chats, gentle strolls and fully recovered we talked of a return home.

'Come across to Waiheke,' suggested Kevin. 'I'll tag along with you in my yacht so you'll be okay if the wind blow up.' It was the casual remark typical of New Zealanders, both in regard to timing and optimism. He did follow us, but we'd already reached the channel between Waiheke and Ponui when he caught us up – about three hours and 20 kms later. The Firth of Thames might be fine for larger yachts but I'm pretty certain it's not advisable sailing for a twelve foot open dinghy.

We spent the night in his house, eating paua fried in butter for the first time and on the following morning were picked up at Kawakawa Bay by Jim O'Brien, pleased that he wasn't having to drive to Thames. He waited while we chatted with a local farmer who gave us permission to leave Ronaki in a paddock close to his house.

Many times after that we met with Kevin. He took us to Warkworth in his yacht, 'Mistletoe' a renovated mussel boat. He'd rigged up a sort of 'heads' for Di consisting of a bit of tarpaulin and a bucket. We sailed over to Kawau Island and finally back to Waiheke where we caught the ferry to Auckland. In those days the ferry was a two to three hour journey – depending on the weather – in an old-fashioned tramp ship with seasoned travelers below drinking and the rest of us up top hoping the agony would end before we vomited.

When I'd finished building Tess – much later – Kevin gave us a couple of small jibs for when we went out in stormy weather. An unlikely scenario. We weren't that daft. Kevin, to round things off, married one of the aforementioned ladies and moved with her to Christchurch. We kept in touch by swapping Christmas cards. At eighty-four Kevin divorced his new wife. Correspondence thereafter was through Betsy. Kevin lived until he was ninety, and Betsy died two years ago (2017) having survived the Christchurch earthquakes.

Other notable events were a coach tour of South island. Amongst a comprehensive tour, the most memorable event occurred in a Dunedin hotel. We had a room on the second floor of a three-storey hotel and had been instructed by the coach driver to assemble in the foyer at eight o'clock in the morning. One of us, probably me, had forgotten something and instead of using the stairs I decided to use the staff lift, illegally, to reach our floor. We stepped into the lift. I looked around at the notices and controls. I dismissed the notices forbidding various things and eyed the controls.

'Seems simple,' I told Di.

And it was. A lever operated a pointer indicating three basic instructions, Up, Down, Stop.

Confidently I swung the lever to Up and obediently, up we went. Numbers flickered past on a screen. One, Two, and going further. Oops! I turned the lever to Stop. And we stopped about six inches above the floor.

'Piece of the proverbial,' I boasted to Di, pushing the lever to Down. We descended, stopping six inches below the floor.

'We can step up that distance,' said Di.

'No. It'll only need a slight push and we'll make a perfect arrival.'

So I twitched the lever to Up and it came off in my hand.

The lift progressed upwards. Visions of crunching into, and then through, the roof flashed through my head.

'Get it back!'

I shoved the lever back on and turned it to Stop as we passed the third floor.

We left the lift there and walked down the stairs in silence having climbed a step about a foot deep to get from the lift. We retrieved whatever had been forgotten and then proceeded to the foyer, again by the stairs.

'Right,' said the courier/driver brightly, 'let's hit the road. Lots of things to do today.'

Milford Sound, the Homer Tunnel, Fraser Glacier; that horrible moment in Dunedin when the lever detached itself. It is the last I remember most vividly.

Skiing on Ruapehu happened courtesy of a school trip organized by Dorothy Smith a founding member of the Rangatira ski club and chief set designer of the Onewhero Drama Society. She's worth a chapter to herself but I'll leave that until later. Suffice to say sliding down the snow-clad slopes, even of Happy Valley was a joy Di and I had never before experienced.

School was a bundle of fun. I'd organized a Soccer XI with Robin Calthorpe as captain, I was in the staff relay team on Sports Days, grabbing the baton on the corner of the third leg and opening up an impressive lead on the inside lane, I related well with all the young people, even being the organiser of a Maori choir. I taught History to small classes of Form Five and Six students. Goodness alone knows why but Disraeli and Gladstone were important parts of the Form 5 History syllabus. However there was a New Zealand component, fairly microscopic so I could read it up overnight. There was also Social Studies to third and fourth formers and Maths to whatever lower age group needed a teacher. What I really wanted to do was to teach Maths to the top classes.

So in 1964 I undertook a Pure Maths Level One course by correspondence at Massey University. Out of an initial intake of over forty, only two of us passed, me with a C+. But I was pleased. I admire those who pass exams, working away by themselves at nights and weekends. C+ was fine. There was no way I could have made an A so slogging my guts out to get a B compared to having a bit of spare time achieving a C pass is a course I seriously commend to all. In fact I felt I might have overdone it with the plus.

I'd also, about half-way through our three year contract, come across the plans of a 16 foot double canoe which I'd bought in England about the time I started my National Service. There had been a vague hope that Lesley would build it while I was in Idris but, not unexpectedly, she didn't. Then there was Sheffield. Finally Graham Bale asked me if I had anything I'd like to build in his evening –class and It occurred to me that there were a number of streams entering the Waikato just asking to be explored by canoe; so 'Simone' joined 'Ronaki' as part of the Carter Fleet.

She was a Hartley designed canoe with a large open cockpit long enough for two people and luggage. Originally she was clad in canvas and, tied to the top of the sidecar, would be transported around the locality and saw service mainly down (not up) the Waikato. She still exists, now a fearsomely heavy vessel clad in fibre-glassed plywood that takes four strong people to lift.

Finally, I must return to the Maurenbrecher family. The eldest daughter, Wilhelmina but known as Noes, was in Form Four when we arrived at Onewhero. Somehow the three of us, Di, Noes and I resonated. She'd arrived in New Zealand unable to speak English and maybe she felt a bond to others who were immigrants, possibly unused to the kiwi culture and more in tune with European customs. Whatever the reason, we clicked and it was largely through Noes that we entered the Maurenbrecher circle and family.

I think she held a secret crush on me. I used to return her home after an evening at our house and she'd sit on the back of Pug, eschewing the sidecar. I'd give her a chaste kiss on the cheek and she once complained about the lack of warmth.

'I am married,' I pointed out gently. 'You're friends to both of us. Let's keep it that way.'

It was an evening such as this that, when I kicked the engine over, it again burst into flames. Noes dashed down to her house while I searched for the litre of water I carried in the sidecar. Ton arrived, panting, and raced into his garage, emerging with a fire extinguisher. It wasn't really a surprise, Ton being one of the most meticulous and efficient men I've known. What was a pleasing discovery, was Ton's inability to use the implement because he couldn't read the instructions on it.

I added my old shirt to the water and waded into the flames while Noes dashed back for Ton's glasses.

The flames were out before Noes returned.

'We'll have a whiskey,' announced Ton. So the three of us trooped back to the house, a beautifully constructed wooden dwelling overlooking the river Waikato. Ton had built it himself.

'It's a Glenfiddich,' he announced proudly, handing me a glass.

'I had something called a Tom Collins in Idris,' I replied and recounted the sessions in the clubhouse after sailing. 'But really I don't know much about whiskey.'

Ton looked at me and nodded. Then he smiled. 'I like honesty. Some people pretend they know about good whiskey and they wouldn't now a good scotch from the cheap stuff they brew down south.'

And from then on Di and I were accepted as part of the Maurenbrecher clan.

It was Henny who found the old shirt where I'd discarded it. She washed it and it was returned to me via Noes.

That last Christmas holiday in N.Z was a mixture of sadness and anticipation. I can't honestly remember what we did. I know I didn't want to return to England apart from the promises we'd made to see everyone 'back home' when the contract had finished.

Di was excited and keen, but me? Well, I at least got her to agree not to send all our stuff back. I bought some crates and packed what I could into them, including Pug. Three large crates were left in the house with our names and the address of my folks in England stenciled on them. Kath said she'd see they got sent if we decided to stay in the UK.

Ronaki and Simone went to Jim O'Brien with the understanding that in the event of our return we'd have them back.

And lastly, the animals. Ossie was left to her own devices. Gruff and Hannah went back to the Beggs. We put them one side of the fence and left and they ran bleating alongside it until they found a gate and leapt over. With tears streaming from our eyes we took them over a farm bridge across a stream. And then blocked the bridge.

'If they get over that, I'm staying,' I muttered.

But they didn't.

Di had arranged for us to return to England overland, on a Penn's tour, but we did our own Onewhero tour first.

Heaps of farewells.

'You'll be back,' Jim told me. 'Anyone who stays in New Zealand for more than eighteen months always returns. The women want to see family but it doesn't take 'em long to realise their mistake. We'll see you back.'

We were, in a way, taking a bit of New Zealand back with us. The doc confirmed that Di was pregnant.

Chapter Sixteen. Going home

Plane to Sydney; then a ship to Bombay. I excelled myself by being sick at anchor in Sydney harbour. This condition lasted three days but was tolerated by the discovery that the surface of the swimming pool remained in a horizontal state.

Following Di's advice concerning the expulsion of carbon dioxide from the blood by deep breathing, I won a competition for retrieving rings from the bottom of the pool. So in one way or the other, the pool plays a significant role in my memory of that part of our journey. To be honest, I can't think of anything else.

And also, honesty compels me to query some parts of the account in reference to the Indian bits. It appears we caught a train to New Dehli; then flew back to Bombay and thence to Karachi. Seated in front of a word processor in 2018, I fail to see any logic in this but Bernadette assures me that Di would have insisted on seeing the Taj. Female thinking she calls it and added that I shouldn't try to understand. I feel vaguely ganged up on.

I am going to quote directly from the log, written on the 28th Jan 1966.

'India dropped beneath us. You get sick of beggars, sick of having to bargain with poverty-stricken wretches whose livelihood was at stake — who desperately needed to sell in order to survive. You get tired of being the rich tourist, tired of tipping, tired of swarms of match-stick kids with hands out-stretched. Sick of the contrasts...It was blissful sinking into the arms of the Alitalia jet.'

Now there are beggars on the streets of Auckland.

A couple of my poems come to mind.

THE PERSIAN DESERT.

In the distant blue, black mountains stand
as islands in a brown and barren ocean.
And sand is scuffed by camels heading
out upon that sea.
Lone hamlets battle cold and wind and heat,
their owners, penned in mounds of mud and straw,
scrape the ground for blades of grass.
Scrawny sheep, black goats search
around the tussocks.
A white-clad figure waves.
The wires and sandy track and railway line keep close.
A comfort in a harsh and unforgiving land.

A NEW ZEALAND VALLEY

To the nomads give the desert,
to the sailors give the sea.
Let the airmen fly the open skies.
Give the thinkers infinity.
But God of land and stars and oceans.
I pray of Thee,
Guard that green New Zealand valley
and keep it safe for me.

It's easy now to see our return to England would only be temporary.

The countries flashed past the window of the coach. And most nights we'd sit at a table in a hotel and I'd write down our adventures - of the constant search for places to pass water and waste , 'ladies to the left of the bus, gentlemen to the right,' of Di's increasing pregnancy with a resulting increase in the number of unscheduled bush stops.

We had a day in Petra, spent a week in Jordan as a result of a revolution in Syria. We became such a frequent part of the local market place that the stall-owners no longer harangued us.

We got lost in Venice and were returned to the hotel by gondola, met up with a teenager in Isfahan who wanted to improve his English. He took us to his house where we sat on a deep white carpet, drinking tea from small glasses his mother brought to us and listening to his collection of Beatle 45's.

At Baalbeck we watched the 'Sound of Music'. It was in English but had Arabic and French sub-titles.

In an attempt to feel less like pupils on a school trip Di and I had early made the decision to find our own accommodation wherever the coach stopped. This led to an inadvertent stay in a hotel in Damascus which in the morning we discovered to be a brothel. Seemed the concierge rented us the room – admittedly a rather gorgeous affair with a provocative décor – because trade was slackening.

Gradually the scene outside the windows was transformed from brown sand to snow-capped hills, from a parched landscape to green, fenced fields, from a crumpled history of fallen castles to the bustling roads where cars and buses did not compete with cows and camels.

We disembarked outside the Penn offices in London. The trip – I hesitate to call it an adventure – was over. Three months had been shared with twenty five others. Naturally we swapped addresses. And naturally we did nothing about them. We did remember to detach the metal tray we'd bought in Isfahan from the spare wheel. Rob now owns it.

Chapter Seventeen. England 1966 – 1967

Loaded with brass jugs, a carpet, the metal tray and a heap of dirty washing we descended on my parents who had now moved very seriously up in the world.

Dad was now the manager of a hundred acre sports field in Southall. The position included a house and apart from over-seeing the various playing fields he was also responsible for a pavilion and a vast amount of sports gear. Although hurt, Di's parents accepted our decision – actually Di's who could cope with her mother less well than she could cope with mine – to remain with my folks until the baby was born.

Dad's chief assistant was an old mate called Bill Jordan. He and his wife Rose had a house next door and both she Mum, worked as cleaners in the pavilion and dressing-rooms. The Jordans owned a couple of small dogs and Dad and Mum had Sally Two, an energetic border collie. It was a happy and prosperous set-up.

I checked in with the local Education Board and spent the next three months relieving at Selbourne Secondary Modern School for Boys, meaning that there was no Form Six. Education finished when at the end of Form Five. It was a surprisingly pleasant part of my teaching career. The staff was almost entirely male. There were a couple of women, I think, because there was a separate women's staff room where they made tea at interval and brought it to us on trays.

Another chauvinistic trait was caning. Most of the men had served in the armed forces during the war. They had been given a short induction course and then let loose into the classrooms. And I know what you are thinking but I'm sure the structure and discipline of that school gave those boys an enviable start to life. They knew and accepted boundaries.

I oversaw a black and red mark system. This entailed totting up all the merit and demerit marks handed out during the week and discovering the winning house who would be awarded...well something. The guy in charge of the house that usually won was rumoured to belt any boy who contributed more than three black marks.

En passant, I feel that mixed schooling doesn't benefit either sex and it's probably more detrimental to boys.

Di was admitted to Middlesex hospital in August and after her 36 hour labour, I witnessed the arrival of Rob, hauled out by a sweating surgeon. I'd been with her most of the time, going home for a wash and then returning to hold her hand, to watch the strain on her face and in her eyes. Eventually the surgeon said they had to get the kid out. Everyone donned white overalls and masks. I was told roughly by the matron that if I keeled over I'd just be carted out of the theatre. It had taken us much argument before I had been given permission.to be present.

Di was lying on the bed staring upwards at the ceiling. I held her hand and gave a running commentary.

'He's just laying some surgical stuff. There's a -'I almost said dirty great big, but stopped myself in time - 'syringe.' I saw him flourish what resembled a large fire extinguisher, 'and a er... '

What he now held was a large pair of pliers the size of a pair of garden shears each blade ending with a hemisphere about six inches in diameter, 'sort of pliers.'

'Push,' said the nurse. Di squeezed my hand. I saw her eyes cringe with the effort.

'Push.'

The surgeon inserted the pliers.

Di panted. The surgeon heaved.

'Coming.'

And Rob arrived, his face red, his head misshapen, his body microscopic. I kissed Di's forehead.

'It's a boy,' said the nurse. 'Leave us now. We're only cleaning up.'

I returned on the bus. 'It's a boy,' I told Dad. Mum was at work. Dad smiled, went to a cabinet and fetched out a bottle of whisky.

'Cheers. Got a name?'

'Robin.'

Amazingly for us, because we seemed to argue furiously at least once a day, the name was decided without rancour. I suggested 'Robin' as one of the few boy's names that had, for me, only pleasant associations. Robin Calthorpe was the captain of the first soccer team Onewhero District High school had ever entered in a local competition, a gently-spoken, hard- working, conscientious lad with a cheery smile, a good sense of humour and very good at Maths. Years later I heard he was farming up North with his partner, another lad.

Then we added two other names, 'Michael', because it was traditional in Carter circles to include the father's Christian name and 'Hans' in memory of Ton's brother who was lost at sea while trying to sail back to Holland single-handed. His boat was found on a reef off the Australian coast but his body was never recovered. Henny consulted a psychic, who said he'd been washed overboard.

Thus burdened with the awesome name of Robin Michael Hans Carter we displayed him to Di's family in Birmingham. Di's mother said, 'Why on earth did you give him a girl's name?' And added that she'd always hoped for a girl. Untactful.

Mrs Pountney – Irene, but I always called her 'Mom' - and I got along famously. We could argue about current affairs, religion and politics without becoming emotional about them. Di seemed to harbour grudges going back to childhood when the clashes about money and clothes and independence loomed large and insoluble i.e. no money, second hand clothes and fights about the right to go off as a waitress to acquire cash.

Hey-ho, I was the male who could do no wrong. Pop, though got his pound of flesh. He'd welcomed me as a future labour force when I'd first visited Birmingham and any return no matter how brief usually involved a ladder, a pot of paint, guttering or sawing up logs of wood.

Usually, the weekend we arrived would involve a family gathering – Aunt Pat, who'd lost her fiancé in the First World War and never did marry, her friend, Aunt Bella, also single, was an adopted aunt and Aunt Nell who'd bring along husband, Uncle Norman. These were sisters on Irene's side. Pop had a brother who's shot off overseas under suspicious circumstances. Di later tried to track him down, after all 'Pountney' isn't a common name, but the only 'Pountney' she found ran a prestigious girls' school in Auckland and who denied all knowledge of any relative.

What with one thing and another most of our time was spent with my folks until September rolled around and we moved to Berkshire where I'd been offered a post teaching Maths at Hungerford Comprehensive School.

Teachers can mark the passage of years by the schools they've taught in. There are exceptions, I know. Some remain in one school most of their lives. And some even return from university to teach in the school they'd been a pupil in. I certainly remember various periods of my life by recalling the young people I taught, the fun times, the nasty times.

Staff: The principal at Hungerford was a young guy, still in his early forties. He let the head of Maths, a Mr Pottle take me around the school.

'The Head's okay,' he said. 'He doesn't like you to smoke in class but he doesn't mind you popping out into the corridor if you're desperate.'

Mr Pottle was a heavy smoker. He'd also been pretty poorly because he'd succumbed to some disease associated with drinking unpasteurized milk. It seemed he'd bought his milk from the local farmer straight from the vat. All the local villagers who'd persuaded him of the financial benefits of missing out the middle man had built up an immunity he lacked. It was hinted that a job as Head of Maths department was mine for the waiting.

Although offered a house on a council estate in Newbury both Di and I thought we'd prefer to live in the country. After Onewhero, town life would be difficult. If we were to make a go of England, green grass, trees, cows, those were essential.

'We'll mosey around and find something ourselves,' I told the Head. 'Thanks for the offer.'

About five miles from the school we discovered the 'Lodge', a miniscule cottage occupied in by-gone days by the gatekeeper. He guarded the gates for the manor house further down a drive and an even larger farm-house at the end of it. It was, what's the word... cute: also cold, the walls being only one layer thick and the doorways so low even I had to stoop to get through into the bedroom which was somehow up a couple of stairs. The windows iced up in winter. But the three of us lived and survived in it for almost a year.

Socially we were isolated. Obviously I had the school staff for company. The day's high-light for Di was when the mail lady delivered a letter. Our status fell between the people further down the drive, the manor-house man commuting to London in his Daimler, and the pig-man who slouched up the drive periodically on his way to the pub. The later we would gladly have befriended but he would have none of it.

'Ah yerrs, ah; we'll ah'l be on me way.'

While living with my folks we'd acquired a Mini-Morris van we named Archie. It originated from a friend of Pop's and in it I learnt to drive and later, almost at the cost of our marriage, taught Di. It allowed us a freedom Di said she'd have gone bonkers without. Archie was green, had bits of decorative wood outlining the rear, cheap to run and to us, used to packing life into a sidecar, spacious.

School was fine. I enjoyed teaching Maths and tried out a system involving splitting the class into groups. This failed lamentably and even Mr Pottle felt obliged to suggest I adopt a more formal approach. Three events stand out in my memory. Firstly a run-in with a fourth-form boy and the situation became intolerable, me yelling 'You're a bloody nuisance.' Possibly true but not good.

Mr Pottle again saved the day by moving the lad to another fourth form class and gently suggested alternative approaches should a similar situation reoccur. 'Take a deep breath or pop out into the corridor for a fag.'

The second incident saw me vehemently defending a lad accused of misbehavior and insolence. I'd even pleased his parents at an interview by stating I'd always found him quite the opposite especially over the previous week. This cheered them enormously until it was pointed out by another member of staff that the lad had been absent that particular week. Closer examination showed I was thinking of the wrong person.

The third blunder involved a transition class. This was a class leaving school at the end of the year and lacking in much motivation to do anything but drive the poor sod teaching them insane. I had them five times a week.

'Find' em something active to do,' suggested Mr Pottle. I discussed it with Ann Booys, a member of staff who was supporting her husband at University in Cambridge.

'Build something.'

I chatted it over with the Head and we decided to build a concrete path. 'Work out what you need and I'll see it's delivered,' he said.

I had no idea how to set about building a concrete path but with the number eight wire mentality I'd experienced in the previous three years felt that even without Google I should be able to do the job. The path was thirty yards long, five feet wide and should be about six inches deep and the ingredients – sand, grit and cement had to be in the ratio of 4:3:1. The original quantities of sand, fine gravel and bags of cement I had worked out as necessary proved much too little and were used up in the first week. It was stupid thinking small.

So I did some more calculations and a couple of trucks dumped their contents on the grass beside the potential path.

In a letter sent to me by Ann when I was safe in Onewhero, she informed me much of the piles still existed and had been named 'Carter's Folly.'

Despite the mistakes, school was fine. The children were similar to those I'd known in Onewhero. I was happy there. We could have made Hungerford our home if it hadn't been for the class-system that had existed long before we arrived. It was the 'Royal County of Berkshire.' Horses were its livelihood and its relaxation. Sure, we'd encountered it in London before we went to New Zealand but we'd lived too long amongst farmers who owned million dollar farms and could be found sweating life out beside their workers in a shearing shed or a milking-shed; at parties you'd rub shoulders with some of the locals who worked for the council on the roads, and sing raucously to a Maori freezing-worker playing a guitar. Okay, it wasn't perfect but hell, no-one, but no-one thought they had more right to be around than anyone else. Not so sure about these days though.

The turning point came when my Aunt Gladys visited us. We'd driven out into the countryside on a sunny day in April – Di and me, just about in our thirties, Rob not yet one, and Aunt Glad, a spinster in her sixties. I pulled into the edge of a lane by a green empty field its road boundary marked by a broken wire fence we stepped over.

On a small rise we looked over the downs of Berkshire, at peace with the surroundings and our small family.

'You're on private land. Get off it'

'But...'

'If you want to argue, the master lives in the house down the road. Have it out with him. He doesn't like trespassers.'

Silently we left. I could feel the rage churning inside of me. I can't remember what the guy looked like but I can recall the smugness with which he wielded his authority.

It was a turning point. The following day, after a pleasantly uncontentious discussion with Di, I bought the Times Educational Gazette and discovered the New Zealand Ministry of Education was still seeking applicants from the UK. Further investigation turned up vacancies in Onewhero District High School.

After a brief correspondence the three of us were invited to appear at New Zealand House in London. The New Zealand commissioner invited us into his office. He appeared delighted to see us. Rob had his nappy changed on the desk and we were told we satisfied all the criteria needed to be accepted as assisted immigrants despite it being our second paid trip. This was marvelous news. We'd already planned to return whatever; being assisted was a major bonus. We told this to the Commissioner who said the whole thing had been sealed by glowing tributes from Onewhero whose Board seemed to have anticipated our return and kept a position vacant by employing a series of relievers. We would, however be obliged to remain at least five years.

'You can make it twenty,' said Di. She'd told me that two weeks into our arrival in London she'd realized we'd made a vast mistake. I felt a glow clouded somewhat by the thought of telling our parents.

Still, there was another thing Di and I had talked about.

'Er... about the journey back...' I said. 'Will it be by air?'

'Yes. Of course. Why? Wanting to swim?'

'We wondered if you'd give us the equivalent in money as you'd spend in air-fares and we'd make our own way there....sort of visit places. We promise we'll be there at whatever date you want.'

'No problem we'll work something out. Just get there by September 8th.' The people in New Zealand are incredibly trusting, pragmatic, and filled with common-sense.

We signed various bits of paper, packed up Rob's nappy bag and floated back to Hungerford.

There were no recriminations from Hungerford School. The head wished us luck and told us he'd always thought we'd be returning to New Zealand. Mr Pottles, who was retiring, wished us all the best. We swapped addresses with Ann and Dave – we still keep in touch with cards at Christmas – and confessed to our folks that this time we were leaving for good. As you'd expect, they accepted the news sadly. Within five years, however, all four parents had joined us and three of them, at least, told us they were grateful for the move.

There was only the problem of concealing the means by which we had determined to travel. We both felt there'd be nasty words spoken if we told them we'd bought a tandem bike with a sidecar attached and proposed cycling across Canada.

In the end, we let Pop into the secret as we'd need someone to bring the car back for us. Inevitably that meant telling Mom but we managed to keep it quiet from my folks until we were safe in New Zealand.

There weren't many good byes to make such as a couple of family parties and a few handshakes. Farewells to the farmer who'd rented us the cottage and to the mail-lady who said she'd love to go with us.

Then we filled Archie with the necessities of life on the road, strapped the bike and sidecar on top, and with Pop alongside me and Di and Rob crunched up in the back, we set off for Liverpool.

Chapter Eighteen. Journey back to New Zealand.

Foolishly forgetting the experience of travelling on a liner, we'd booked a tramp steamer which slogged its way backwards and forwards between Liverpool and Montreal. So two days were written off, filled as they were with an inability to hold anything down combined with a robust child who still needed feeding at two hourly intervals.

We recovered sufficiently to glide through flat, grey waters for a couple of days before slipping into the harbour at Montreal. It had become a pleasant and comfortable trip. The other six passengers, some remaining aboard for the return passage had been interested in our proposed journey across Canada with much discussion and many suggestions. Rob and his well-being figured large in people's minds and the absence of toys compelled the engineer to make him a rattle by placing ball-bearings into a tin can and welding the top back on.

As we entered the docks, I attached the sidecar to the tandem, its position on the right conforming to the Canadian driving code, something I'd realized and prepared for before we departed. We offered the purser a tip but he refused it, remarking that he was sure our needs were greater than his. Then we packed the sidecar with everything we couldn't get into the carriers on the front and rear of the tandem, somehow squashed in the lad and set off down the gang-plank and into the bustling traffic of Montreal.

It took two days before we were headed on the right road. Disaster almost struck at our first round-a-bout which we started to negotiate in a clockwise direction. Cars swerved violently, horns blew.

'Shit.' We hurriedly dismounted and pushed the outfit in the correct direction, Rob standing up in the sidecar and waving to drivers who by and large treated the whole thing as a welcome joke. We encountered a bridge and the local sheriff escorted us over it, one of his cohorts driving in front while he protected our rear. Behind him stretched a line of cars.

About midday we stopped, ate, played with the lad and looked around for somewhere to erect a tent. This basically became the structure of the day. Sometimes an hour of cycling would be added in the afternoon but not often. Usually we'd find a farm and pitch a tent under some trees with a couple of interested kids and a farmer's wife watching with interest. One place we found was really poor. Fences were bits of sticks tied together. The loo was outside the house and when we peeked inside found it was a hole in the ground which was pretty close to being filled.

'Ed's gonna close it up soon and dig another one,' explained the wife, vaguely apologizing. 'Next coupla days I guess.'

Another time there was an horrendous storm and wind. A tent pole snapped and I splinted it together with a tent peg, Di holding up the roof as I did so while the lightning zig and zagged across the night sky and the rain came down in torrents.

But the following day was fine and we dried out the tent during a gloriously inactive few hours before thanking the farmer who'd popped across to see how we'd survived the storm and then pedaling on our way.

At a dreamy little settlement we were stopped and were asked to give a short talk on the local radio frequency about how wonderful Canada was and how we were enjoying the clean air and exercise. Di concluded our enthusiastic spiel by a short plea that if anyone driving a truck saw an idiot family pushing a crazy combination of bicycle and carry-cot, to stop and pick us up. No-one did. Although a couple in a village asked us if we had a monkey in the funny box attached to the bike.

'Good heavens, it's a baby. Hey, Elba, look it's a kid. You must be....' She paused and we left her searching her vocabulary for a suitable word.

The initial supposition was that we could manage fifty miles a day and in the two months at our disposal we'd cross the continent in time to catch our plane at Vancouver on the 5th of September well in time to start at Onewhero on the first day of term 3. We'd been over-optimistic.

Firstly we'd taken too much. I disposed of writing materials. Bang went the log. That's why this account isn't going to be terribly reliable. On successive days we wrapped up most of our clothing and dispatched it by mail to Onewhero. Finally we had a change of underwear, a spare shirt between us and the shorts we wore. The rest of the space was devoted to Rob's essentials – spare nappies, clothing, his tin-can rattle, milk bottle and food.

Secondly, the state of our backsides, unaccustomed to being rubbed by narrow leather seats for hours on end, took ages to harden up.

Thirdly, Rob just couldn't cope with being tied into the sidecar for hours on end. We'd try to set off early in the morning, get five miles under our wheels while he was still sleepy, stop for a meal and then push on until he started complaining about life and expressing displeasure by heaving oddments overboard.

Also we'd decided the whole plan was stupid and we'd never manage to cover the whole continent – 3000 miles at an average of twenty miles a day. We'd scarcely be in Vancouver by Christmas. We consulted a map and ended the first part of our Canadian trip at Sudbury on the banks of a Great Lake. Here we caught a train on which we spent three days and two hideous nights before reaching Banff at the foot of the Rockies. Thence to Vancouver.

Before disillusion set in and we were no longer on speaking terms with our fellow passengers, we were asked where we were heading. 'Auckland, New Zealand.'

'Gee, I didn't know you could get there by train. What's it like?' He was serious.

Rob had constipation. Both nights on the train were spent taking turns to carry him up and down corridors trying to calm him down as he passed microcosmic sized pellets. The days weren't much better. Everyone was relieved when we disembarked at Banff.

The Rockies loomed before us.

Ten or so miles from Banff we found a camping ground where we pitched the tent on a wooden platform, being given a hammer and nails for the task. Camping on the ground wasn't permitted. This was something to do with the prevalence of bears, a consideration outside our expectations. We were told not to feed them.

The next day saw us sweating our way up the mountain pass towards the Pacific. We walked up for two days stopping in a car-park where we encountered a couple with whom I still correspond. They fed and wined us and we refused the offer of a lift, firstly it would involve separating the sidecar from the tandem and secondly because we felt a moral obligation to do the last few hundred miles on our own wheels.

We reached the summit and spent the next couple of hours sweeping downhill towards the aptly, for us, named township of Golden.

Wonderful! We'd come to clear air and sunshine. But, heck; one stop further on I noticed a spoke in the rear wheel had fallen out. Ten minutes later another one lost. We limped into Golden very carefully minus six spokes. The first thing we did was search for a place that sold and repaired cycles.

Al Ruttan charged us half a crown for the repairs and nothing for letting us spend the night in his garage with the heater going full-blast. I swap Christmas cards with his wife Liz even now (2019) but it's unlikely that the long-standing invitation to visit New Zealand will be taken up. Maybe a grandkid might come a-knocking.

Then on to Vancouver alongside train-lines running through steep gorges, the roads filling up. A bicycle shop offered to buy our outfit, excluding Rob, but we foolishly rejected the chance to save on the expense of bringing it with us on the plane.

It was a talking point momentarily in Onewhero. We actually had our photo on the back page of the NZ Herald while on a trip to Putaruru to visit a step-brother of Noes' and later took the tandem without the sidecar to South island. Finally, however those pieces of our history disappeared. I gave the tandem to a boy in Te Kohanga to encourage his attendance at school more easily. It didn't. The sidecar slowly fell apart after becoming a chook nesting box.

Jim picked us up at Auckland Airport and delivered us to the house in the Kaipo Flats we'd left just over twenty months previously.

We were home.

Chapter Nineteen. 1967 - 1969

Unpacking the boxes we'd left addressed to Warren, Farm Sports Ground, closely resembled the feelings engendered by Christmas. Each box held memories not only of our previous three years in New Zealand but also of the stuff we'd brought from England prior to that.

Of course there was Pug, and Ronaki, and Simone to be reunited with. Alas, not Gruff or Hannah, but Oswald was still around. She was living in the roof and seemed pleased that we had returned, resuming the nightly feeds and caresses.

Lawrie was no longer principal, a position now occupied by a Bob Davies who also had children at the school. Fred Woods, the Senior Secondary Assistant was still there although his relations with the new principal were strained to the extent that they communicated only by notes, each believing the other to be untrustworthy.

I let most of the ill-feeling float past. Di and I had our own family now and despite all the pain of Rob's birth, Di was talking of adding to it - apart from some more goats that is. After all the trauma and distress of a baby's delivery, it amazes me that any woman can contemplate repeating the ordeal.

We'd resumed our relationship with the district as if we'd merely been away on an extended holiday. Ronaki returned to the garage and with Noes we often spent week-ends at Kawakawa Bay, sailing out to Putaki island and over to Ponui. I had a short item published in the New Zealand Herald about such a trip.

When Rob was about eighteen months old we'd set up the tent, lit a fire and stood on the curling pebbly spit heading out to the Lighthouse all the while keeping an eye on our son. He was standing ankle deep in water dropping stones, a smile spreading over his face as the ripples circled. I called it 'Time should stop.' Corny, and I'm glad it didn't.

My classroom was a happy place for me, and hopefully for my students. Many of those we'd taught in our first years were still there, happy to greet us but now definitely senior school. Noes was a prefect, Carol was repeating a School Cert year and her boy-friend, Keith, had caught up with her. Keith had arrived when she was in Form Four. They had become an entity and were the only couple permitted to walk hand-in-hand around the school. Carol wanted to be a nurse but needed School Certificate to be accepted into training. In those days. In order to get a pass in School Cert. you had to have an average of 50% in four subjects one of which had to be English in which you had to score at least 30%. But most managed.

Actually Carol did pass. She became a nurse and yes, Keith and Carol did marry and are still together.

It's curious how in some years the classes are easier to remember than others. There's the Form Three that we met in 1962 and which left, with us, in 1965.

There are the years when our own two went through the system. It's unfair to pick out separate years and young people. They were all happy years. If I mention any or fail to, call it Dementia or Alzheimer or prudence.

So school bowled along. Graham Bale the woodwork teacher was still there, Neil Ackhurst was there, still occupying the school house, so was Chris Ward who taught French and Tony Webby the art-teacher. Ann Anderson was teaching the infants and Mavis Hatwell the standards. Matt Tawhari had left but it was still basically the school we remembered. But the axe above it was quivering.

Meantime Sally was born and I had an afternoon off school to welcome her arrival.

Pukeohe Hospital catered for both ends of the age spectrum. On 30th July 1968 I witnessed Sally's birth. Compared to her brother coming into the world Sally presented infinitely less trauma. According to Di it was less painful, the hospital staff more relaxed, and the atmosphere of the hospital more of a home than a production facility. It was another good reason to be back in New Zealand.   Forty years later my mother died there in the elderly care unit.

'You won't be up to much housework,' I told Di casually after she and Sally had joined Rob and me in Onewhero. 'So a bit more mess shouldn't worry you.'

Actually neither of us were ever really concerned with mess but she raised an eyebrow. 'So?'

'Ronaki's too small for four of us. I wondered about building a boat. There's something called a Hartley trailer-sailer I saw advertised. I'd be able to build it in the lounge.

I measured it. There'd be sawdust and shavings but it wouldn't be all that messy.'

'Go for it.'

So we have two delightful photographs. One shows Di holding a small red-faced baby gazing at the skeleton of a boat filling a room; another has a serious two year-old hitting nails into the frame of Tess, the boat that figured large in the next few decades both with us and the generations of Onewhero kids who sailed in her around Ponui and down the Waikato River.

Talking casually to one of the fourth form girls about goats we'd had, she offered us two not quite up to some standard her father considered viable. So for a couple of years we had Annabelle and George. Annabelle enjoyed sleeping with Sally in her pram on the verandah. Both goats disappeared mysteriously. I suspected a local lad, possibly protecting someone's garden where unfortunately the goats couldn't discriminate between roses and weeds. No corpses turned up.

They just vanished.

I've discovered a poem I wrote on 21st April, 1969:

"The gentleness of sleep on a son's face,
the outflung arm, the stillness of his breath.
And in her sleep, she smiles,
and all the beauty that is woman floods her baby
face
A son, a daughter, a wife.
My son, my daughter, my wife.
Thank you for the tempo of the day,
for the games of evening, for the silence of night,
For the reason of living."

Another significant event of the period following our return from the UK was the purchase of a house. There was the possibility of buying half an acre from John Halford, the one married to the Scotswoman, Flora. This section had somehow been separated when a road had been built some years previously. We contemplated buying the house we were now renting from Kath and Nelson Bovill and moving it onto the Halford section. Everyone was agreeable, including the Raglan County Council who would have to sign things off. The local chairman of the School Board, Jack Mitchell, who was the parish representative on the RCC, saw to this.

Then the childless Portellos who lived on the rim of the caldera moved into an aged facility. Their only remaining relatives put the sale of the property in the hands of Cecil and Norah Rollinson. They're the parents of the girl who had hit me on the head with a mallet in

'Irresistible Albert' two years previously. Martin van Vaught who had the adjourning farm withdrew his offer and we purchased a house, a garage and two acres for one thousand pounds.

It was a difficult decision. Jack Mitchell, who'd put a fair bit of work into organizing the Halford section for us, advised us to go for the bigger one. 'Room for a cow.'

The house has an interesting history. Built in 1903, there were originally four rooms. The front two formed the store of a flourishing village named Te Herua which used to have its own hall and milk factory. The hall had occupied a place close to the house but had been removed some years previously and tacked on to the Onewhero hall and used as a supper room and library. The drama club used it as changing rooms when there was a production.

The Portellos had a shed at the bottom of their section where Harry would to milk ten cows although he used the domain when the grass on the section ran out. So we'd a shed as well as the house, garage and an external shack containing some stone sinks and an old copper.

'Knock it all down and build or move a house on to it,' was the most usual suggestion.

Then our potential neighbor, living opposite, came over one day while we were plithering around not really knowing what we should do. Jim Stone was a builder. He and Joyce had three sons and a daughter, all who attended the local school. His son Ross had instructed me in the rules of Rugby back in 1963 when I'd been given a

Form Four P.E. class. I'd enthusiastically joined in the brawls thinking they were an integral part of the game and at one stage had suffered a high tackle.

'Hoi,' said Ross. 'That's a foul.' I broke up the resulting fight but had always had a soft spot for the family. What you give out, you get back.

'Don't be in a hurry to demolish the lot,' said Jim. 'The roof's okay, new iron a couple of years back. Timber's sound – good old macrocarpa. Last another hundred years. You'd better check the piles 'though.'

I was wearing my, 'shit, in the council flats we were only expected to change light bulbs' expression. Ultimately I stuck a crow-bar between the old part of the house and the Putello's living-room extension and pried it loose. The old wash-house was demolished a couple of years later by Ralf, a member of one of those classes that remain fixed in my mind. He jumped up and down on its roof until it all collapsed beneath him.

Re-piling was an art in itself. Many of the piles were riddled with boror and rotten below the earth. Ken Carly, a local farmer who later loaned me a tractor with a front-end loader to get rid of a flax-hedge – 'this lever'll raise and lower the bucket. It's easy. You can't go wrong,' – demonstrated how to use a house-jack to raise the floor of the house so as to remove the old pile, dig a hole and cement a concrete block in.

Then with a small level, about the only precision instrument I possessed, I would wiggle it around until the block was horizontal in all directions before placing a water-proof liner on the concrete block to protect the wooden pile. This was cut from a length of six by six which I usually had to re-cut because I'd been scared I'd cut off too much, then I'd cut too much off the pile and have to make-up for this with additional bits of liner. And finally twiddling the jack lever and hearing the old house sigh gratefully as it sank onto its new pile. Di and I between us could manage to do five piles in a morning while Rob and Sally would mess around in a pile of builder's mix.

I might as well finish the saga of the house while we're at dealing with foundations…. Ken told me I ought to make the underneath of the house, flooring, piles, everything, boror proof by spraying it. This time we bought a sprayer and while Di stood clear of the house and pumped' I crawled beneath it with a length of hose spraying everything, including myself with a not unpleasant but definitely pervasive mix of creosote and kerosene.

The back of the house was replaced by Monty Mason who was on the School Board. He decided the new floor would have to be a step lower than the old one as he needed a really horizontal line to work from and my jacking hadn't quite fulfilled that prerequisite.

We moved into our new home in 1970 thus becoming a definite and permanent part of the district.

The house has constantly evolved. Ten years later, with our children wanting a bedroom each, I cut a hole in our bedroom ceiling, lowered the ceiling, cut a hole in the roof and built a new room. The local building inspector kept an eye on the whole process and a student Maths teacher built some stairs. I had intended having a ladder, but the inspector told me the new room needed more than four inch nails attaching that to the old bit. The front door was changed from dull green to sparkling yellow, Di's favourite colour. Yellow curtains dangled in front of most windows. The old scrim covering planks of macrocarpa were covered firstly with hardboard and later these in turn with tongue and grooved macracarpa which gave it, we hoped, a polished, modern interior.

Did I mention buying the flooring to the new back of the house from the demolished remnants of the old Waiuku primary school, or the hours spent punching down protruding nails so that I choked myself sanding down the new (and old) flooring? Or inveigling visitors to join us in painting vast areas?

We met the Purves family on a trip to Coromandel after Rob and Sally had left home. Dave and Shona had four girls ranging from Lindy at 11 Kirsty 9, Jennifer 7 and Helen 2. We took the older three up Castle Rock for the afternoon while Dave went fishing and Shona took Helen to the dentist in Thames. We've watched the girls grow up and one visit they helped paint the roof.

'Dad would never let us do this,' enthused Jennifer clad in an old pair of overalls, slapping paint onto the corrugated iron.

'Too dangerous?' I wondered. 'Don't go to close to the edge.'

'No,' answered Lindy, 'He said we wouldn't be good enough.'

'Just get the stuff on. But don't fall off the roof.'

And on another occasion an ex-teacher, John Biggs, arrived with a group of cousins. It eventuated they were all at a loose end so I dashed into Pukekohe and bought enough paint and five or six brushes, rang Jock to borrow his water blaster, sent Di back to Pukekohe for beer, lemonade and food and over the week-end managed to get two coats of paint on three walls of the house. The front wall, protected by an admittedly slowly decaying verandah roof hasn't received any new paint since, I guess, 1903 when the house was built.

Chapter Twenty. 1968 – 1989

These years were our family years. Rob and Sally went to Onewhero District High School where Di taught them General Science at Form 3 and 4 and later Chemistry and Biology in the senior school. She was a part-timer with a permanent job at the school. We were grateful that she combined the roles of mother, wife, milk-maid, egg- collector, rooster killer so well with the hours she put in at school. Di also managed to fit in time to be the school board secretary for years.

Somewhere along the line we collected Mash, a loveable largish brown and white female mutt who had been left in Jim and Joyce's care when the boys and Anne left home. For months she would potter across the road and join us in whatever we happened to be doing. She eventually accompanied us on caving expeditions, sailing trips, tramping trips with the school, but at home she was content to play with the kids, joining in mad dashes around the sort of bar I had constructed in the kitchen after I'd been told to put in something to hold the roof up. Or just lying in front of the wood range with the Rob or Sally or the cats sprawled on top of her. I'd return her to Jim in the dark, clip her chain on and kiss her goodnight.

'This is daft,' I told Jim one day. 'Why doesn't she just stay with us fulltime?'

And so she did. From 1978 until 1986 she was a constant companion, hauled up rocks deep underground, standing precariously on a wind-surfer, fighting for a place on a bunk in a forest hut. She was over fifteen when she accompanied me on a walk along the Hukanui stream from Coromandel to Coroglen where Rob picked us up. She was so tired I had to carry her over the last stream and when we reached home I lifted her onto the settee and she stayed there for over twelve hours. Writing about Coromandel reminds me of another camping highlight she and I shared.

Learning the clarinet is not a soothing experience for someone listening and in the interests of domestic harmony I had taken myself, my clarinet, a music stand and Mash into the depths of Coromandel to practice in isolation. Some years before there used to be a designated track to a 4 bunk hut near the turn-off to the Hukanui river flats. This section of the track was no longer maintained.

With Mash at my heels I pushed my way along the overgrown track until I found the hut, still with a roof and bunks and we spent the night there. The following morning I set-up the music stand, assembled my clarinet and, accompanied by an occasional howl from Mash, my renditions wafted off amongst the trees.

Suddenly, from the tangled mass of trees and undergrowth surrounding the hut, a figure burst, throwing herself at my feet and exclaiming, 'Thank God I heard your music.'

Not an apparition, but a genuine tearfully grateful young lady who had departed the actual track and found a few markers from the one that had been discontinued. Wandering deeper into the Coromandel forest she became progressively disorientated and scared. Then, magically... the uplifting tones of a clarinet in a duet with a dog.

It was one of those moments few musicians have experienced.

Mash, the wonder dog, was ours for seven years (1976 -83). In the end, one sad afternoon I took him to the vet and then brought him home back for burial under a tree in the garden. Mash had a wake at which many folk in the district attended. I got drunk on whisky donated by one of the hard-nosed farmers there.

Rob and Sally grew up with Mash over their teenage years. It's one of those awful truths that dogs grow closer to you as they age, children grow away. Mash died about the same time both our son and daughter were in the process of leaving home. Sally went to university (1984) and Rob into the theatre and then travelled overseas.

I left full-time teaching about that time, too.

Chapter Twenty one.
Education, family, construction, and trips.

In 1970 the Ministry of Education decided the County of Raglan needed a new secondary school. Pukekohe High School, with the Intermediate almost next door was bursting at the seams as they absorbed the students from Tuakau as well as Pukekohe. Another high school was imperative and Tuakau the obvious choice for one. The major problem was what was to be done with the secondary department of Onewhero District High School.

There were a number of options. The first was to turn Onewhero into a primary school catering for the local kids. Another was to make it into an Intermediate accepting students from over the river – Te Kohanga, Pukekawa, Glen Murray; or it could stay as it was, a District High School; or it could become one of the new type of schools, an Area School which offered a seamless education from new Entrants to Form Six (Year 13).

Anything other than the last infuriated the Onewhero community who wanted nothing to do with a new school at Tuakau. Nothing wrong with the education offered at the District High School, it was maintained; these young people in the back country areas travelled far enough as it was; in any case, said under the breath, 'Who wanted to mix it with Tuakau?'

Politics entered the equation. Onewhero was a wealthy, farming area, and almost to a man and woman, supporters of the National party, definitely not a group to be ignored.

Instead of informing the Onewhero community that the secondary education of their children would be at Tuakau and that since most farmers sent their sons and daughters to either Kings or St Cuths, it really wouldn't matter to them, the government decided to let the various districts affected vote on what they wanted.

Tuakau unanimously voted for a Year 7 – 13 school at Tuakau. Te Kohanga and Pukekawa voted less unanimously to support this. Onewhero voted with only one exception (we all suspected the principal) to support the status quo while working hard towards translating into an Area School.

The Ministry hoped the Onewhero resolve would collapse and there would be a steady stream of secondary-aged pupils to the super new school over the river. They were wrong.

In 1974 Tuakau College opened and immediately offered a free bus service to any students from Onewhero who wished to use the facilities of this new educational institution. Some did, but six years later a larger bus was put on to transport pupils from Tuakau and Te Kohanga to Onewhero. A number of the Onewhero secondary staff were persuaded to take up positions at the college with the threat that if they didn't accept the positons offered they wouldn't get a second chance. Hewi Tauroa, the first

Tuakau principal, talked of a snobbish white separatist group on top of a hill.

Of the Onewhero secondary staff only Di and I remained, helped out by June Mcoubrie and shortly, when our numbers didn't decline, the Education board appointed a succession of newly qualified teachers, much needed but didn't have the mentorship they sorely required. We also had a number of principals whose experience was purely with primary education.

I was given the position of Senior Secondary Assistant, which in the circumstances didn't mean much. Essentially for the next seven years a dedicated few led by me and Di kept the secondary department alive until the Education Board gave up and Onewhero District High school became an Area School.

It wasn't easy. In the light of my C+ from Massey I taught mathematics throughout the school, even, at one stage taking a combined standard 2,3,4 class, a combined form 3and 4 class and a combined Form 5 and 6 class. That year, I remember, the last period on Friday I had the whole of the secondary department – all 26 of them – in my classroom for a combined Maths class. I was responsible for the timetable – which involved a 7 period day, each period being 40 mins long. We started at 9 am had a break at 10.20, and then another couple of periods ending at 12 noon. An hour's break and three afternoon periods before the buses rolled up to take everyone home at 3 o'clock.

It was a 35 period week. Typically it would, for me, involve 20 periods of Maths, 6 periods of English, 6 of

History, a Music period and sports or P.E. and a free period if I was lucky.

I'd often take a combined Form 1 and 2 (now Years 7and 8) class in exchange for one of the primary department teachers working in the secondary area in Art or Social Studies. This was one of the advantages of the District High School set-up which became the model for the Area School.

The roll for the secondary department was eighteen at one stage but had climbed to over forty by the time we translated to an Area School. For almost seven years we existed not knowing if the axe would fall and we'd all be moved to Tuakau College. We became a family. Those years were the hardest but probably the most enjoyable of my teaching career.

It was during the seventies that two major mathematical changes were made. Firstly the decimal system spilled over into the currency, weights, and measurements. Just for the fact that I can still remember them: four farthings made a penny, (think of it a cent), a halfpenny was two farthings, twelve pennies made a shilling, two shillings made a florin and two and a half shillings was half a crown, although a full crown didn't exist.

Twenty shillings made a pound. Twenty-one shillings made a guinea. To think we used to teach all that stuff! There were the weights too in empirical measurement - ounces, pounds, stones, hundredweights and tons. Fluids also in the old way; and linear measurement. If you dispensed with all the time those calculations needed you had to find something to fill the vacuum.

Presumably that's why New Maths was introduced. I thought it wonderful. Suddenly numbers made sense. And because it had to make sense to me before I could teach it, I think I was a better Maths teacher for it. Anyway, my classes seemed to enjoy the subject and there's a letter from someone in the Auckland Mathematics Association asking me to give them a talk. I turned it down.

One of the advantages of the smaller class numbers was the ease of transporting the whole lot in cars. I had often thought that the idea of having school trips at the end of the year, although a pleasant way of keeping the young ones happy, missed the opportunity of useful bonding. We compromised by establishing the tradition of school trips at both ends of the year.

To save repeating a trip I devised a roster of outings. Over the three years any pupil would be in my care, she or he would have six trips. This, by the way, was before our numbers warranted a Form 6 (Year 12).

The trips rotated sometimes around parts of Coromandel Forest Park and Kaurenga Valley. There was Moss Creek Hut, the Pinnacles Hut, and a clearing somewhere before Coroglen. On one occasion the girls organising the trip hadn't rationed our food properly and the last night saw twenty-four of us sharing one loaf of bread.

Canoeing the Waikato from Cambridge to the Tuakau Bridge was another trip. We had a motor boat accompanying us and on one occasion had two which was fortunate since they alternately broke down and had to tow each other periodically. We in canoes refused towing offers.

A major flotilla of Onewhero craft would depart from Kawakawa Bay and sail, motor, paddle to the northernmost point of Ponui where we'd spend the next few days eating oysters or mussels. At night we'd sit around a blazing fire and sing songs, while a frying pan holding a freshly baked griddle-cake was passed from hand to hand, bites taken out of the nourishing fare as the still-warm pan went around the circle.

Some years saw all the horses in the district rounded up and a four day horse-trek organised. To me they were the most nerve-wracking trips I've ever been on. And the occasion when I sat on a nag which would only trot, the most uncomfortable of all gaits.

Another trip was to Waikaremoana where we once took a heap of donated cabbages which we swapped for trout caught by green-starved fishermen.

There was a small lake called Waikareti in the same area whither on one occasion we walked   carrying canoes and sacks of vegetables. None of this dried stuff for us…. Boredom actually set in the second day and a ranger at the hut named Bill offered to take us for a day's walk. After six hours he said he'd see if he could find out where we were and walked off. An hour later, after the whole group of us had almost gone hoarse shouting 'Bill', and 'Help' he reappeared and led us back. Seemed he was a ranger but not local. He was from Wellington.

Once we walked through the Kaimais from Waikino to Katikati, crossing several streams, stopping at a couple of huts and emerging from the bush to meet the trucks and cars returning us to Onewhero.

'All aboard?'

'Yes.'

And at Onewhero a solitary rucksack proclaimed that we weren't. One boy had been left engrossed in a comic in the loos at Katikati. An unpleasant call from the police sergeant there brought me driving back but by the time I arrived they were so pleased to get rid of him that I was looked upon as a saviour rather than an irresponsible idiot.

We walked from the Mangetepopo Hut across to the Ketatahi Hut in summer and winter a number of times. Bathing in a hot pool of water with the snow drifting down onto your face is an experience now, alas not available. Mind you running back to the hut afterwards was a bit teeth-clenching.

The Ketatahi Hut gave us quite a scare once. After attempting to out-scare each other with tales of the Tongariro monster a Maori girl suddenly went stiff: her eyes rolled back so only the whites were showing.

It was snowing. We bundled her up in blankets, put her between me and a mother who was on the trip. Sometime in the night I heard her sigh and her body relax. Wonderful. That was the night Rob fell out of the top bunk – there were three tiers. Fortunately one of the parents who insisted in carrying his own camp-bed, was underneath and broke his fall.

Rob and Sally started coming on the trips from the age of six and four. It got so that trips lost their novelty. Rob kept on until he left school but on one notable occasion Sally refused point-blank to go.

I had given my usual spiel to everyone – and their parents if they were still reluctant. A couple of sixth-formers whose parents had succumbed to my arguments about the benefits trips offered, approached me irately when they discovered Sally wasn't going.

'Why, isn't she on the trip, like we have to be?' Bryce demanded.

'She refused, ' I explained. 'And her parents couldn't get her to change her mind.'

Sally had started school at the age of four. Di was needed as a part-time teacher to cover some of the Science classes. She said she'd do it on condition Sally would be accepted in the new entrants' class. Sally had always envied Rob.

I clearly remember the first day Rob accompanied me to school. He and I went on Pug, Rob in the sidecar. An infuriated three year old was left screaming at the door.

'Why can't I go? I can do anything he can.' Up until the actual time of our departure she'd quietly dressed herself, collected together a bag of pencils and seemed completely reconciled to being left at home. She wasn't.

Life went on. Di's folks had arrived in New Zealand in the late sixties and mine shortly after. Pop had retired and he and Irene rented a cottage in the Kaipo Flats. Mine found a house on the Klondyke road, rent free if Dad would keep an eye on the stock. So N.Z. introduced him into sheep and cattle management. Dogs supplied. The two sets of parents provided immediate child-minding opportunities, and mine often took Rob and Sally away on holiday with them —especially to Whitianga which they made a yearly holiday destination.

Dad, bravely in my opinion, gave up pension rights and the probability of retirement accommodation in the UK to start a new life. He found work immediately with the Pukekohe Council, his first job being to assist in chopping down a number of trees. However he swiftly rose to being the head groundsman, helpind design and maintain the new Pukekohe stadium, now home to the Steelers and constantly being consulted on bowling and cricket greens.

Mum reveled in not going to work. When Dad retired at 65, they looked around for a house of their own and Mum managed to organize a small cottage moved onto our section. It was the first and only house they had ever owned outright and they were very proud. Having my parents so close upped the child-minding stakes although over the years my mother and Di started or possibly increased a mutual dislike that spilt over to include Sally and put horrible strains on me.

'She never liked me. She was jealous because she thinks I think I'm better than she is because I've got a degree,' Di would exclaim.

'You're more intelligent. Rise above it.'

'You always take her side.'

Di didn't really like her own mother either. Me, I'm the eternal compromiser. I can't avoid seeing the other person's point of view. There are times when I envy those who have deep convictions. The deepest conviction I have is that no-one really knows the ultimate truth about anything.

Irene missed her family back in Birmingham. She stayed because she wouldn't leave Pop who loved the role of a local identity. She never felt at home here. The first time she went paddling at the Port, her sandals were swept out to sea. She spent much of her time in bed, reading and died in 1974. Pop seemed proud of the fact that he took her ashes back to England and sprinkled them in the sea at Devon where they'd spent their honeymoon. I thought she might have preferred going when she was alive, but who knows?

Dad retired in 1973.....the moment he turned 65 and lived until he was 91 enjoying the freedom that Di and I had found in N.Z. He renovated, built, gardened, drove Coley, their VW Beetle, and toured the countryside dragging a collapsible trailer. Which brings me to another major occupation of mine. And as it's my autobiography I'll list my own achievements in the building line.

Di and I early started looking around for an income not dependent on teaching, not because it wasn't enjoyable but because I'd heard too much of teachers, especially males, dying of boredom shortly after retirement.

We bought the section over the road belonging to the Presbyterian church for $4000 and put a cook's cottage on it. This was a roofed and walled shell. With Dad's help I made it into a rentable cottage and then a sizeable chunk of cash when it was sold. This involved designing the interior rooms, toilets, plumbing and lighting. I found this relatively easy and thereupon decided to design and build from scratch, a small cottage on the section we owned on which had once stood the Te Hirua hall. This was a heady leap. With my experience of teaching Technical Drawing to a Form three class, I drew up a set of plans and presented them to the Rodney County Council.

The building inspector was scathing. 'Have you looked at building requirements? You must show dimensions of the studs, the piles must be of a legal height. What are the spacings between beams?'

Chastened, I discovered a book covering the current building code and decided that I might as well make the house two-storeyed.

'You'll never do it. Two storeys is beyond you,mate. Stick to something single.'

The third set of plans was drawn up. 'Oh build the bloody thing,' said the building inspector. So Dad and I did.

It's still there and rented out at $140 a week, a useful addition to the benefit. I helped Dad with a garage for his trailer and that is still erect although their house has gone. We sectioned off the bottom bit of our section and sold it to the Lorimors. Scott married Jess who is the daughter to Dori and Rick Muir and although there's a couple of surveying pegs, neither family takes much heed of the boundary between the two sections.

Sometime in the seventies or eighties, still intent of an alternate financial income I had a discussion with Di and we ventured into the world of horticulture, building three hooped plastic-covered tunnel houses. This was eminently unsuccessful. The initial plan of growing tomatoes, with all the lateraling and tying that involved was quickly rejected. Rob and Sally weren't too happy either.

They had been physically involved in building a large water tank, a necessary prerequisite of any horticultural project. The day before Ralf and a team were due to pour concrete into the hollow blocks from which the tank was constructed. Golly, our cow, in pursuit of her calf, squeezed between the wall of our garage and the newly erected tank. The top three layers of blocks slumped. The gentle evening we had planned, disappeared as the kids mixed cement and spread it onto the blocks as Di and I lifted them up into place.

It was finished with the light from torches, by about eleven o'clock.

To conclude the horticulture venture... tomatoes were replaced by grapes and these possibly paid their way (but not ours) until the Australians flooded the markets; apart from this, a tunnel house cover – four hundred dollars' worth of plastic coagulated into an inseparable mess while we were having a cup of tea Mum insisted we have before it got cold, and another plastic cover blew itself into shreds despite my bringing my sixth form Maths class up to attempt a rescue.

I can recall the chat I had with another grape-grower.

'The bunches must be pruned, don't forget.'

Me, 'I know. The bunches need space to grow.'

Grower, ' No, each bunch must be pruned to the right shape.'

So grapes disappeared down the gurgler too.

We sold one tunnel house to Rick, a neighbor, for the cost of the galvanized tubing, and I gave most of the straight lengths to Pete to help with the various hangars on his farm. A bit of one still remains. I envision a cricket practice net for a future Black Cap.

The mention of hangars brings up yet another activity occupying much of our time and cash. Flying. This probably merits a new chapter.

Chapter Twenty two.
Flying, dramatics, music, and soccer.

There's a distinct memory of walking from school to the bus-stop chatting with a mate, Nobby Clark. We'd looked up at the contrails left by the plane across the blue summer's sky. 'I'm going to be a pilot when I leave school,' said Nobby.

I shrugged. 'With my eyes I'd never be a pilot but I'd like to be a navigator in a bomber.' The war and its stories were still fresh to both of us. Incidentally Graham Bale told me he'd been a navigator on Lancaster bombers during the war.

They'd been hit and three of them scrambled for the door while the pilot was yelling to them to get out. Someone got jammed and before he could be shoved out forcibly the plane righted itself and they all stayed with it. And one month they had two leaves one after the other because the station had lost six planes one night and as leaves were given in strict rotation, their second leave came round the day they returned from the first one.

However, .I had lost touch with Nobby and despite national Service in the RAF I was only airborne as a passenger until 1972, by which time tension existed in our marital bliss.

By this time Di and I had our own home in Onewhero. We had Rob who was six and Sally, two years younger. Our parents lived close by. The school was beginning the battle for survival. We'd been married eleven years. We snarled at each other over the smallest things.

I can't remember the cause of the argument but it concluded with me storming out and driving to Auckland where I sat in a café and thought things over.

I returned. 'Sorry. I've been thinking. I reckon we're bored. We need something we can do together which is exciting and different.'

Di heard me out and the following weekend we drove to Ardmore where she signed up for pilot instruction and I joined the Auckland Parachute Club as it was then called.

I was proud of my wife. She'd never for one moment contemplated flying a plane but during the next six years she became a fully licensed private pilot, started studying for a commercial license, had ratings on Cessnas and Austers and watched as I'd jumped out of planes. In those early days of round parachutes with panels removed to facilitate steering, landings were definitely a spectator sport. I've landed in a pig-sty, countless back-gardens, a tree…. And occasionally in the DZ (drop zone.)

I had one occasion on which I cut away my main chute and deployed my reserve. I'd left the plane successfully, tiddled around doing flips and things – it was called 'style' but I just liked playing birds. Not of course that birds do backward somersaults…. Anyway having reached 3000 ft I pulled the rip-cord handle and, looking up, noticed a line had managed to cast itself over the canopy, virtually making it into a gigantic bra. Methodically and moderately excited, I cut the whole thing away by releasing two catches and then pulled the rip cord handle of the reserve. This I then, in the required sequence, threw away. The reserve just sat there, possibly wondering what it should do after all this time shut away from any activity. Eventually, I grabbed a handful and chucked it out. (A short while after this a pilot chute became mandatory on all reserves). All this took time and space and what with there being a hill I only had about ten seconds float-time before I landed in the tree afore-mentioned.

It took ages to untangle the canopy from the branches. Di had to ring the School Committee of which she was secretary, to explain she'd be late for the meeting scheduled that evening. She was guilty of exaggeration when she said I was still in the tree.

Rob and Sally hated Ardmore Airport. We'd bring toys and books but planes quickly lost appeal and scanning the skies waiting for me to appear wasn't all that gripping, although the time someone just ahead of me hit powerlines, was. He survived, with burn marks on his shoulders but the two young women who on separate occasions plunged earthwards with the reserve entangled with the main, died. I wrote several poems about parachuting. Here's one.

TO MARIA, died 23 August 1975

Somewhere above the green landscape,
cut by dark splashes of bush,
With the narrow winding river curving its passage
to the sea,
she knew that the earth rushing towards her
marked off the seconds of her life.

With a tangle of two canopies spinning her
uselessly,
with people staring, horrified and numb,
she plunged down.
But we have all counted those odds,
weighed them against the friendships
Of a small cabin a mile above the ground,
Weighed them against excitement,
the joy of flying on a magic mattress of air;
And the gentle grace of a parachute descent;
and weighing them,
Accepted the bill that is always,
somewhere, presented.

And while I have my book of poetry open, here's another one:

CLIMB TO JUMP HEIGHT   written 10th July 1975

The ground is hard at fifty feet,
no contours cushioned by height,
But there is a touch of magic at five hundred feet,
and the air has a sharper bite.
From a thousand feet it's a kids' playground
of midget dips and hills,
Soft green lakes and matchbox homes
and time which is almost still.
From a mile and a half you gaze
across a blue-domed canopy.
You see the coast and mountain merge
into the grey and wrinkled sea.
At two miles high in blue cold air your feel,
The land is beyond comprehension,
and only the sky is real.
And now it's jump height;
a moment's pause at an open door,
Until with outstretched arms you soar
Into concertina'd time.
You see the figures drift across the sky,
You float, you laugh your fall, you climb,
You swim you dive you turn,
you cry a shout of joy as you fly –
a lifetime in a minute.

Years and years later – well, at least thirty – this became one of the songs a group of us put together on a disk entitled 'Blue Skies Dreaming'.

My old-fashioned round parachute was declared obsolete in 1979 and I was told to buy one of the new square canopies on the market or give up. Di had already decided flying had become too expensive – the cost initially had been $8 an hour but was now in the region of $50 – so for the next 13 years I existed earthbound.

There was always dramatics. The Onewhero Drama club put on a pantomime each Christmas and I, after being the Dame for a number of years and then one of the pair of idiots each panto demanded, decided to attempt writing one. The first was 'Cinderella'.

Despite contrary advice I insisted that Cinderella arrive at the ball in a coach drawn by a live, miniature horse I'd discovered in a paddock owned by the Lobbs a large family of six which I had once taken home all together, quite irresponsibly, letting them hold on to various parts of the motor bike and sidecar.

I was assured the Shetland pony was docile and eminently suitable for a career on the stage. Practices proved this to be true but on the opening night it rained and, unused to the temporary awning we had erected, it bolted through the door way, across the front of the hall until the carriage collided with the door way opposite. The groom, a brave man, raced after them. Cinderella picked herself up and to the cheers of the audience climbed onto the stage. I think it was one of Donna's greatest achievements.

Incredibly we repeated the horse and cart part of the performance for two more nights without untoward occurrences. It is possible the financial success of the production was due to the bloodthirsty expectations of the audiences.

Where was I? Dramas. I wrote a version of Peter Pan, a new slant to accommodate three ladies who desperately wanted roles. They became the Three Wild Ladies of the West; I had them popping up in various spots, and even gave them a scene to themselves. Incidentally we wrote the music as well. I'd write the lyrics and a coterie involving Bridget Eady who played violin in the Auckland Philharmonic, Keith Masemann whose eventual arrival at Onewhero in 1978, was the final blow in the Education Board's attempts to close our secondary department (although straight out of training college, not only did he know his stuff, Keith could silence a class with a glance) and Di, Rob and Sally, wrote the music and amended the lyrics to fit. Once we sat around the table vaguely humming tunes. Suddenly inspiration came. I selected two sets of letters the letters A-G from a pack of alphabetic cards, shuffled them and dealt out four. 'They're the first four notes.'

Then I sat back, my contribution finished. Bridget leaned forward. 'De, deah, de, dah,' and smiled. And they were away.

I directed other productions, and acted in more. Rob preferred playing music but Sally and Di preferred acting.

By the time Sally was eight and Rob ten they were both good guitar players and Rob had started teaching himself the banjo, left to him by Pop (Di's dad). Sally was skilled on the fiddle. Di had been taught piano as a youngster. She added guitar to her skills. Me? I struggled with the recorder, graduating from descant to tenor to bass and finally clarinet. I still remembered the Welsh principal telling me to keep quiet. I found the concept of chords impossible to get my head around.

Rowan taught a composite Standard 2,3,4, class in the primary department and for a couple of years taught Sally and Rob. As with many teachers, we invited him home and he quickly became a frequent guest. Both Rob and Sally told us they didn't learn a great deal of Maths or English but Rowan would spend an hour a day playing music to the class and they loved him.

Able to play anything with strings, Rowan passed me over an old mandolin. 'A clarinet doesn't suit Bluegrass,' he explained.' So I learnt a few chords and strummed away having the chords written down over the exact word before I could play it.

At the age of ten, Rob could tell me all the chords of 'She'll be Coming Round the Mountain' just by thinking the tune in his head. Sally had discovered by herself how harmonies worked.

Still I struggled. I wanted desperately to play music. This is, of course, the basic prerequisite. So many people have told me, 'I really don't understand all those squiggles and things,' referring to sheet music. 'It would be nice to play music, but I've never tried it.'

To which I reply, 'Do you really want to?'

Similar to the answer to those parents asking me how to get their children to read. 'Chuck away the television.' Of course they never did.

I'm no virtuoso but I can thump out chords more or less correctly in the more or less required places. I can tootle notes on a clarinet or recorder and blow out noises on a blues harp. I'm not a session musician like Sally, I was never as knowledgeable as Di, I'm not as instinctively accomplished as Rob, but I enjoy playing music and have reached a level where the relatively indiscriminating majority of listeners think I'm okay. It is my contention that anyone who positively wishes to reach that sort of level, can. You don't have to dedicate your whole life to it as the top players do. But, while practising here and there, particularly with others, you'll have fun.

Still on that subject, I went from recorders to a clarinet and shortly afterwards discovered its tuning was different from most other instruments, being B flat. Uncle Google will explain. A wealthy son-in-law bought me a C clarinet which helped, but essentially I was stuck with either playing my Bb clarinet from music or playing entirely by ear. I selected music squiggles, ultimately joining a local orchestra where I became a 2nd clarinetist. I eventually took a succession of exams reaching 5th grade level in the Trinity College syllabus.

Playing for the 'Pukekohe Melody Makers' was interesting and not without its lighter moments. Sitting by the stage peering up at the local lasses performing the 'can-can', the 1st clarinetist whispered into my ear, 'that chick second from the end, I don't think she's wearing any pants.'

There was the time during a rehearsal of 'South Pacific' when Anita, the set designer, was painting a back-cloth and while we were practicing 'Bali-Ha'i,' the island appeared on the blank canvas as if by magic. And the rehearsal where one of the brass section (they're the nutty ones) produced a clockwork model of a trombonist, and it pottered across the stage under the conductor's nose the instrument waving in the air.

Being second clarinetist often involved counting for thirty-odd bars before playing a couple of notes and then relapsing into a semi coma, unless of course girls were dancing the can-can. I drifted out of clarinetting and when Rowan gave me a mandolin, I stuck with that. It's a much more social instrument. I've now joined a ukulele group in Tauranga and found the ukulele easy to play, eminently portable and good to listen to.

Over the years I'd taught myself to play the mouth-organ starting with a chromatic one I bought from one of the soldiers transiting through Idris on the way to fighting Egypt in 1956, and ending with my collection of small Hohner Blues harps in a variety of keys. And just as I went from recorder to clarinet and to mandolin, retaining some knowledge of each so, ten years ago, I suddenly was awoken to the potential of the blues Harp. I discovered the pentatonic scale. If you sucked mightily, not only did you produce the whining 'blueish' sound, but you could play in a different key!

See Uncle G if you don't understand me. If you do, you'll understand my excitement. It took almost fifty years for me to learn this.

Chapter Twenty three

The years as a family of four, five if you include Mash, and heaps bigger if you count the cats, various lambs, hens and Golly, the cow whom, as a calf, we swapped for a bag of cement, flashed past.

Rob and Sally, from sleeping one above the other in a set of bunks I'd constructed – the top bunk, occupied by Rob was so close to the ceiling he nailed a cushion to a beam to preserve his skull – got separate rooms after I'd added a room in the attic. Rob had the front room, Sally the one off the lounge. Di and I were upstairs. Most evenings seemed to involve visitors, often to play music, otherwise because they wanted a chat. We didn't own a television set a fact neither Rob nor Sally have regretted.

In any case, they could always pop down to my folks if they wanted to watch something. The first T.V. Di and I owned was one inherited from my mother in 2003 and it occupied a cold separate room so was only available if you were prepared to sit inl discomfort.

Most Auckland Anniversary weekends were spent at the Folk Festival. It was here that an Irish fiddle player taught Sally to love Irish music and another year Sef shot off home to fetch and then give her his old black fiddle.

Yet other family weeks were spent on Tess, the sixteen footer I'd built. We'd always spent part of the Summer Holiday sailing – Bay of islands or Coromandel or around the islands near Waiheke. We'd come into an anchorage with me yelling instructions, Di on the helm, Sally standing by the main-halyard preparing to drop the main sail, Rob poised on the bows ready to heave over the anchor and me half in and out of the cabin ready to heave up the centre -board.

'Stick her into wind, now.'

The plan was seldom executed to my satisfaction. Sometimes Tess' bows went through the wind before the jib-sheet, the responsibility of the helmsman/woman, had been released and Tess hurtled off on another tack or we'd got too close to shore and the centre-board had to be pulled up causing a sideways drift onto the beach. Or maybe the main halyard had become entangled with a stay or the anchor got dropped too soon and ... ah well....memories. I prefer to remember the evenings on the beach around a campfire with singing and chats and, dare I say it, the occasional whiff of cannabis. Especially when we'd brought along others less conscious of the law than we were. Or of an evening sprawled out in the cabin playing monopoly or up and down the river, and Mash with her legs sticking out at 90 degrees to her body taking up much more than her fair share of space.

Eventually Di made an awning which we draped over the boom and Mash had the cockpit to herself. She also occupied the first dinghy I built when we came to appreciate how useful this would be ferrying goods and people ashore from a boat moored out in ten feet of water. Unfortunately my design, although it could float was on the small side. Until we later bought an aluminum one, for a couple of years people peering at us from more palatial yachts would see four people swimming alongside, and occasionally clinging to, a small tub occupied by a couple of haversack and a dog.

Tess was the main component of many school trips too, loaded with rucksacks and cartons of food and, on one notable occasion, three large bits of rusty steel which, we were assured, when heated in a hangi pit, were the modern equivalent of stones

One of the most stupid things I ever did happened while sailing Tess with three fifth form boys in Coromandel harbour. We were transporting a heap of gear to a beach where Ian James has permitted us to pitch tents. Being towed was 'Blossom' the small dinghy which had replaced the rubbish thing I had built. On it I had strapped, inexpertly, a large surf board. In the middle of the harbour this detached itself. I immediately stuck Tess' bows into wind and held her there, giving instructions to someone to swim over and retrieve the surf-board. No-one accepting this invitation, I expressed my disgust, 'load of whoosies, just hold her into wind.'

Then I tore off my life-jacket, knowing how much of a drag it would be, leapt overboard and swam towards the errant board bobbing amongst the waves. As I was climbing onto it, I saw Tess' bows turn gently to one side, her sails fill and she drew away slowly, but with gathering speed. 'Hoi,' I shouted, standing on the board. 'Turn the tiller...the stick at the back'

I envisaged Tess transporting the boys into an unknown fate. Maybe Waiheke....no, impossible, surely they'd be able to ask for assistance? And what of me, what would be said to me floating in the middle of Coromandel harbour on a surf-board without a paddle, clad only in a pair of swimming togs?

Well, fortunately Sam jammed the tiller over, the boom cracked across without hitting anyone and they bore back on me, slinging over a bit of rope on the way past.

No sooner had we all recovered our nerve than we saw Jock, sailing another loaded trailer-sailer steer straight for the beach and then, to our astonishment, right up it. However it transpired one of the stays had unscrewed itself and tacking had not become an option. All things considered the school trip could only get better.

Another memorable sailing event took place amongst some substantial waves in the Ponui channel. Rob, Di and I were on a catamaran with me at the helm. A piece of rope dangling over the bow of the port pontoon caught my eye. 'Could you get that Di, please?' She crawled forward and reached over as I saw the wave approach.

'Better come back,' I amended, 'there's a wave....'

'What's that?'

'Doesn't matter.'

The wave banged down and Di and the port pontoon were submerged. Rob futilely going to assist his mother was projected outwards. With, I thought, commendable agility, I managed to be standing on the starboard pontoon still relatively dry when the heads of my wife and son re-appeared.

'While you're there,' I said, 'you might as well swim over and grab the rudder and centre-board.'

Mike Wright rescued everyone in the motor-boat.

Talking of Mike Wright, he was with us on a trip to Stoney Batter where a series of subterranean tunnels are an ancient defense reminder of N.Z.'s vulnerability against nautical invaders.

We motored and sailed across to Waiheke, moored up and went ashore. On reaching the entrance to the tunnel we discovered we hadn't brought torches. Fortunately a group of students were playing 'Dungeons and Dragons' and one offered us a candle and a box of matches. So we explored the tunnels in a long line, each hanging onto the shoulders of the person in front. It was a scary journey and when we ultimately reached daylight again Mike said. 'God what I would give for a beer.'

And there, at the entrance/exit was a bottle of beer. Which he drank feeling that something in the way of a miracle shouldn't be ignored.

Parents and friends were always encouraged on school trips and occasionally joined with us on an Easter or Summer holiday.

It was when Rob and Sally were 10 and 8. I'd earlier swum ashore and managed to borrow a more substantial rowing boat than Blossom feeling she wouldn't handle the large breaking waves near the shore. Di didn't fancy the journey ashore in an overcrowded rowing boat so she was watching while I rowed the kids and Ralf who had joined us for the trip, up to the breaking waves.

I'd worked out my strategy. I would row with the stern facing the shore, feeling the waves lift up the bows. At the right moment I would swiftly turn around the boat and surf in. it all depended on immaculate timing. I heard Ralf's voice, sort of hoarse.

'Mike!'

I looked over my shoulder. All I could see was a wall of water. I glanced up and saw the tip of the wall disintegrate into a white cascade.

The wave swamped then sank, the boat. We all swam ashore, holding onto it, floating alongside us upside down.

Surprisingly few words were spoken, not from us, nor the onlookers, nor the boat's owner once he'd discovered his craft was undamaged. In fact the only casualty was Ralf whose left boot had come off and was never found.

The birth of Berk Award was announced in Te Kohanga. It is presented to someone who comes up with an inane idea. I received it in 1973 with the suggestion of a mid-winter raft-race across the river. We were each allowed a large cube of polypropylene. These we mounted one cold evening in the middle of June. They all promptly capsized and proved impossible to remain on, let alone steer.

'Stupid, bloody Berk.'

Tony received it from me for trying to fly Sally on the end of a bit of rope and after that...who knows. And maybe Sally's trip tied into a parachute wasn't the occasion for Tony to be recognised as a certified Berk but it does allow me to return to the years of family.

They were coming to a close, rapidly. Rob had always enjoyed the theatre and he ultimately achieved his ambitions ending up as lighting designer in theatres in London, New York, Helsinki.

He started with the Onewhero Drama Club, branching out into puppetry where he built his own puppet theatre, designed the puppets, made their costumes and wrote the scripts. He joined the technical side of the Mercury theatre through the good graces of Ilona Rodgers whom he'd helped learn a major role in a play she was in.

He'd needed space for all the puppets so I cut a hole in the ceiling of his bedroom and he spilled up into the attic. And after all the years he's now (2019) making sets and designing lights for OSPA –the Onewhero Society of Performing Arts.

Talking of cutting holes in ceilings, in the early eighties I read in a book about an harmonograph which created wondrous random patterns. It involved two rotating pendulums (pendula?) Perched near the top of each were gyrating gimbals made from some clutch plates. On the top of one was a platform which accommodated the paper, and a pen was attached to the other.

The size of the resulting squiggle, interesting, varied and occasionally erotic, depended on the length of the rods, to the ends of which was soldered tin cans full of lead. John M and I progressed from a table model to a larger one situated in a barn and eventually to the final edition in the hallway of my house, the rotating platforms situated just below the roof, creating masterpieces above the holes in the hall ceiling cut to accommodate the rods. Despite all our efforts the results were not of a size commensurate with our endeavours. Still. It was a fun experiment and explains the rectangular saw marks above the hall. Di was an interested spectator and voiced no concerns about the reconstruction. Mind you I did spend much of my early retirement lining the house with tongue and groove macrocarpa to lend the décor a backwoods flavor. Not ceilings, though.

By the time she was fourteen, Sally was carving out her own life. She left school at sixteen and went straight to University. She boarded in Auckland, living in a large house owned by the local Tuakau doctor, Alec. A couple of years after his arrival as the local GP in Tuakau his wife had left him and we provided friendship and interests outside his duties.

Sally married him in 1985. In 1994 they moved to Tasmania where Alec had accepted the post of a Professor of Medicine at Launceston University. He spent a great deal of time both at work and promoting himself with overseas seminars and lectures unaware of the loneliness Sally experienced. He lavished expensive trips and clothing on her, even purchasing a grand piano which she learnt to play while he was absent. It wasn't enough and they were separated in 1992.

Actually I found Alec okay. I'll relate one of the funniest paragliding experiences in another chapter.

Chapter Twenty Four. 1989 – 2000

By 1989 Di and I were left by ourselves apart from whichever cat had now turned up. My folks were still in their small cottage at the bottom of our section but both of Di's had died, her mother, Irene, in 1972 and Pop in 1980.

Sally was married, and so she and Rob were living separate lives in Auckland.

The tunnel house experiment had proved a failure or rather, an experience without any financial rewards. I decided to try my hand at writing, sending short stories to the School Journal and longer ones to various publishers. Over the years I've had eight short stories published in the School Journal, and two plays. Wendy Pye published a short book 'The largest Pool of All', and In Australia the School magazine published two stories and Lothian Press, before they went broke, published three teenage novels. I entered – and still occasionally enter – various writing competitions, notably one sponsored by the Waikato District Council. In 2014 I won the adult essay about Matariki and Sally who validated her entry by explaining she'd entered her contribution while on holiday here, came second in the Maori section.

I gave up my fulltime position at Onewhero in 1989 when I launched into writing at the age of 53. The plan had been to chug along supplementing the income from writing by relief teaching, until the age-benefit kicked in at 60. This had been decreed by Robert Muldoon but was increased to 65 by a later government in an attempt to balance the books. As a compromise, those of us caught on the hop, as it were, were handed out a reduced retirement benefit at age 63. Our attempts at alternatives to teaching were never successful, financially.

The whole of that diatribe is to explain why the ten years after I left Onewhero Area School were only a sort-of retirement. We still needed to generate income. The State didn't kick in a contribution until 1999 and only by 2001 did I get the full amount. Ditto Di.

I was still playing soccer most Saturdays during the winter season. I'd played for Pukekohe way back in 1964 and 1965, again in the early seventies until a group of us inaugurated an Onewhero Soccer team. This would assemble with the opposition in a local's front room after a home-game and consume beer. Our first games had been played on the horse paddock in the Onewhero Domain and derogative remarks were made of the surface until we dug up the concrete wicket pad in the middle of the school field and played there. Which reminds me.

1972, the year the song 'Great Flaming Balls of Fire' was in the top twenty. I have Form 6 for PE. And we are playing a sort of game of cricket on that self-same concrete pad. Ralf is at the crease and Mary is bowling. Catherine, a tall quietly spoken daughter of proud upright, church-going parents is poised at square leg.

Mary hurls down the ball and simultaneously the bell denoting the end of school rings. Ralf, lashing out at the ball is put off his stroke and the ball thumps into his groin. He falls to the ground clutching himself. The bell stops ringing. Catherine murmurs, 'Great Flaming Balls of Fire,' and we all troop off the field leaving Ralf to crawl after us.

Soccer. Ultimately the problem of scraping together eleven players each Saturday plus learning that the player organizing the purchase of beer was consuming most of it during the week, together with the discovery that Tuakau had started a soccer team prompted us to shift over the bridge. There we played soccer, drank beer and convinced ourselves that we were keeping fit in the process without any administrative duties. My last game, although unaware of it at the time, was in September 2001. I can't remember the result but I was probably injured in it. We did, however on one memorable occasion after three years of never winning a game, beat Pukekohe 3rd XI two nil. They were two players short and had hinted that we should lend them one of our three reserves but we refused.

I coached girls' soccer teams for ages –at Onewhero until I left and then again on and off into the new millennium; I had one six week spell relief teaching at Pukekohe High and had a girls' under fourteen side dumped on me, and at Tuakau I coached the Ist XI for a season when I had two terms teaching there. The coaching, apart from lunch-time sessions, included refereeing home games and escorting teams to away games. For someone who'd retired from teaching I spent a lot of time with young people. Basically it was relief teaching that kept the household running until the new millennium.

I had actually intended to introduce paragliding. I'd read about a parachute that actually soared upwards so, in the summer of 1992, took lessons with Bill at Karioitahi. Three of us stood on a small grassy outcrop overlooking the beach and the sea reaching out to Australia.

'Who's going first?'

We looked at each other and as the eldest and thus presumably the most expendable, I volunteered but not without first suggesting that we saw a demonstration.

'No need,' said Bill. 'In any case I'd have to leave you lot up here while I took off, landed, and then slogged up the hill again. Look, I'll explain, do what I tell you which'll mainly be run like f... when I tell you and keep going even when you've reached the edge.'

These were the early days when the only things you needed to be an instructor were a few spare canopies.

'Okay.' I donned my son's bicycle helmet and some overalls I'd used when parachuting. Bill strapped me into the harness and stretched the canopy out on the ground behind me.

'Hold on to these.' He held up the main straps attaching the harness to the canopy. I gripped them tightly. 'These lines are fastened to the front and back of the canopy.' I noted these. 'Pull the left one and you go left, pull the right one and you go right. Piece of piss. But you probably won't need them because all you'll do is drift slowly downwards and land on the beach. Okay?'

I nodded.

'Okay start running.'

I reached the edge of the take-off area without losing contact with the ground so hauled myself into the air by the straps.

Five seconds later as I picked myself up from a provident ledge a couple of metres below where I'd stepped into space, Bill peered down.

'Hurt yourself?'

'No.' I spoke shortly.

'You shouldn't have pulled down on the straps. Not the front ones, any-rate. That just collapsed the front of the canopy. You'll be okay next time.'

And the second time was good. I drifted down watching the beach approach and after completing an unnecessary parachute landing roll, picked up the canopy and trudged up the hill. By the time I arrived Bill was speaking to the last member of our group. She was a nervous looking young Japanese girl who couldn't speak English well but she was with a boy-friend who could. Bill had produced a pair of walkie-talkies one of which he had given to the girl.

'Cost me over a grand,' he explained as I arrived on the hill. 'Only used when I think someone needs it.' He put the receiver around the girl's neck. 'When I say "left", you pull this. Right?'

The girl nodded, her eyes slightly glazed.

'If I say….', he turned to the girl's boy-friend. 'What's "Right" in Japanese?'

'Rsplkrieojh.' (Or something).

Bill spoke the word slowly to the girl, pulling down on the riser.

She nodded again.

I've taught Japanese students visiting N.Z and know that politeness will always prevail over a confession of ignorance. I should have spoken but, hell, he was the Instructor.

Kamikaze style the girl ran towards the edge and flew away. 'Thank God,' I thought. Bill was speaking into the microphone. *'Rsplkrieojh'* The girl flew on. Bill's voice rose. 'Right….Hell.' She'd reached the end of the sand.

'Christ.' Bill dropped the transmitter and tore off downhill.

'Can we have another go?'

'Yes.'

We watched as Bill reached the beach just about when the girl touched down in the sea. He ploughed out towards her and we somewhat callously switched to the problem of fastening the lines and straps to a harness debating which way round the canopy would fly. 'Openings of the channels to the front or rear?'

Bill recued the girl and gave her a tandem ride out of relief. The girl's half of the new communication gear was a write-off. I'd got the paragliding bug which stayed with me until I switched to engine-powered flight in 1998.

All of that is a prelude to the Alec's possibly unique paragliding experience. Alec, now Sally's husband, on hearing I was purchasing a paraglider from APCO, an Israeli company, told me to get two; he'd like to paraglide.

'Why not try it first?'

He tried it and confirmed his readiness to purchase one.

So now we were on the edge of the Kaipo Flats on a gentle slope facing a steady ten knot N.W. wind. Some twenty feet below from where we were taking off was a two foot high electric fence held up by steel battens.

'Easy clear that,' said Alec. He adroitly flicked the canopy into the air and looking up, checked that it was indeed flying correctly. He'd used up ten feet of slope.

He took a couple of more steps and then realising that the fence was almost upon him, took a neatly delicate jump to clear the fence. This was successful up to a point insofar as although Alec was airborne, the seat of the harness, on which he now sat, had hooked itself under the wire. The wind took him aloft until he was the head of a bow-string made from a stretched electric fence from which all the battens except those at either end had been twitched. He stopped about thirty feet off the ground, peering down.

'What do I do?'

'I've never read anything like this in the manual,' I gurgled. 'Hang on until I get a camera.'

Alas, the line broke and he just drifted away.

Paragliding provided endless joy and excitement. It is truly the nearest thing to being a bird that a human can experience – except maybe hang-gliding, which incidentally Ralf, John Binsted and Tony Maurenbrecher – Noes' brother –and I tried. These were in the very early days and we broke our contraption so many times that it became obvious we would ultimately break ourselves, so it was given away.

Most of my paragliding was done along the west coast on days when the wind blew steadily and not too quickly from the South West. I flew over secluded bays ignoring the grappling couples beneath me, spiraled upwards sufficiently to speed swiftly over gaps in the coast as the up-draught disappeared, had the odd seagull fly alongside contemptuous of my flying abilities.

At Shakespeare Bay I saw a learner fly with great precision into the only tree in sight. I once witnessed an Instructor clutching the legs of his student as the latter inadvertently and unexpectedly became airborne. The pair of them were dragged over the ground, all the time the instructor bellowing incoherently.

Seeing a hang-glider pilot land down-wind is always an interesting sight. This is a venial error usually in the early days but can end in broken bones. The unfortunate pilot sprints along the beach desperately clutching his bar as s/he attempts to outrun the wind until the whole contraption nosedives into the sand and the pilot plunges through the wing into the sand.

Once I took off into a wind faster than I could fly. I found myself drifting slowly but inexorably backwards, sucked into a gap where a small stream trickled over a waterfall. Heads popped up from left and right wondering how it would all end. Actually, I landed gently at the top of the waterfall, the canopy sank behind me and I waved triumphantly to the probably disappointed heads. Then I climbed down to the beach where a dog leapt out from behind a rock, bit me and ran off.

That was the second accident I experienced involving paragliders. In another wind stronger than expected, I took off at the top of the Kaipo Flats and again found myself drifting backwards.

I somewhat stupidly wondered what would happen if I turned downwind to fly across the paddock I had taken off from and descend on the other side. As I shot across the paddock at a wind plus chute combined speed of about 50km/hr I became aware, not only that I was sinking rapidly, but that a wire fence marked the end of the paddock. I envisaged having both legs amputated in a unique and bloody accident.

So I pulled down on one riser and stalled myself onto the side of the hill sloping down to my right.

That I could pick myself up after thumping down on the hill was a miracle. It seemed much of Onewhero had witnessed the whole procedure from various points, mostly through binoculars, so a fleet of cars arrived to see if I had survived. However despite a throbbing leg and foot, both of which by the following day had turned black, I could struggle along upright.

Gay, a St John's leader, told me the foot had heaps of bones and even if I had broken one there wasn't much anyone could do about it, so I used a walking stick for a week or two and got on with life.

The paragliding scene I remember with pangs of joy and nostalgia is one involving Tess – not the boat but a small, part Yorkshire terrier who came into our lives in 1988, two years after Mash died. Grant, a neighbor had been walking his Alsatian along the banks of the Waikato when, amongst the reeds, it sniffed out a sack containing two small pups.

'You're good dog people. You need a dog. Which one do you want?' We chose the smaller blonde one. The Skellams had the other.

Tess was with us thirteen years, another of those beings with whom you share your home and your life and who grows closer and closer to you as the years pass.

She and I walked to the top of the Klondyke hill, Puke o Tahinga, and I spread the canopy out on a flat clearing at the top. By this time I'd become reasonably expert with a B licence permitting me to take-off unsupervised. I flicked the straps so I was facing the canopy, the wind at my back. Then I took a step backwards, saw the wing fill, a large rectangular sail edging on flight.

'See you at the bottom, Tess.' Then I turned around to face the wind and took two steps. The canopy soared over my head and I was off the ground; I swept across the front of the take-off area, peered down at Tess peering up. 'Come on, girl....' And then I was off drifting out from the summit and then down to land in the small paddock next to the farmer's house. Tess had stood all this time, watching.

The next few minutes were anxious ones until I saw a small brown figure start bounding down the hill, crossing a stream, scrambling under fences and around rocks....And we greeted each other with joy and love.

Leonard, a local farmer and prominent member of the Drama club – I'd seen him balance a ladder on two chairs themselves on a table, to adjust some lighting – and of course there was the time we painted the old hall roof, tying ourselves to bits of rope attached to the ground on the other side... Oh yes; at a Calf club day, Leonard awarded Tess third prize in an ugly dog competition and my mother was in tears and never really forgave him.

Digressing - Leonard has a unique role in Onewhero life. Unmarried, he donates a considerable amount of his spare time and cash to Drama, being the largest contributor to the fund which built the new theatre and is in a constant demand as a set designer and builder. He was the one who came into our section with his tractor to dig a large hole where we buried Golly 20 or so years after we'd swapped her for that bag of cement. Di used to walk her up and down our road edge. Golly, and then her calf, Polly, supplied us with milk and cream. Di's apple crumble swimming in cream was famous throughout the district.

'Mike's a lucky feller,' Jock once growled to his wife. 'Crumble and crumpet.'

Tess was Di's dog, but mine when something more interesting turned up. She'd chase me along the beach at Kario while I was flying overhead; she came on Duke of

Edinburgh trips, standing guard at the tent door and letting no-one but family in. She accompanied us to South Island. She had one trip in her namesake and numerous trips in canoes, standing on the bows and occasionally slipping off. I remember driving in 'Newton', our blue ute on the tray of which I built a box which Di and I fondly considered to be a house-truck, and Tess travelling on Di's lap. When we passed the rail-crossing at Buckland and a train came into view, Di would say, 'Look, Bud, train.' And Tess would stare intelligently out of the window in the direction of Di's finger.

Chapter Twenty five. 1998 - 2010 Grandchildren, Australia, the folks, Duke of Edinburgh Awards, canoeing

Life was full, interesting and fun. Di looked after the home front, the house, food, finances. We did a fair bit of canoeing together, looked after Tess, commuted fairly regularly to Australia. Above all we shared music, and over the years played together, firstly in an Irish band called 'Over the Hill' and then in 'Hangar Torque'. We played at three preschools, the Wise Owls Pukekohe, one in Te Kohanga, and the other in Onewhero, Di on the guitar and me doing the actions and singing the words.

Occasionally joined by Donna, one of the four Casey children Rob and Sally grew up with. For the last two years we had together we performed at a number of old-folky type clubs and rest homes, with music and a video of me flying. Those last few years were the closest we'd been for a long time.

It's a truism that the longer you live, the more deaths you encounter. Di's mum had died in 1972; a blood clot. Her father in 1980. He'd smoked all his life and it caught up with him after he'd entered hospital to have his second leg amputated. My dad died from a brain hemorrhage in 2003, and my mother in 2007.

Tess, our lovely Tess, died in convulsions after eating something she shouldn't have. We had her wake and for the second time I got drunk on whisky. The memories flooded back, the trips through the bush, on the river. Me slipping over while carrying her across a stream in the Coromandel Forest park and her running off and Di and me blundering about calling her name until we found her following us; Duke of Edinburgh trips with Tess and Toodles, the dog of Keryl, the Tuakau teacher, guarding their respective tents; of her running down to the folks' house where their cat taught her how to catch and play with mice; she and Rolly our ginger tom having mock fights, paws around each other's necks, claws sheathed and her presence, with us wherever, whenever.

She was with us on just one trip sailing on her namesake to Ponui, and we scared stiff she might slip overboard. A couple of days before she died I remember waiting for Di outside a supermarket and singing 'O Tessy girl, the pipes, the pipes are calling...' to the tune of 'Danny Boy.' To this day I find it hard to stop my eyes watering when I hear it. I recall the number, too many, of pupils I've taught who've died in car accidents or by their own hands; sadly too of cancer.

Chapter Twenty six

At least once a year Di and I would make the trip to Australia. After she'd separated from Alec, Sally bought a house in Launceston and we became familiar with the journey to Melbourne, the wait for the plane to Tasmania and the hour flight to Launceston where we'd be greeted by Sally or her new husband, Jan accompanied, later still, by our grand-daughters, Josephine and Sophie.

In between the visits to Sally we flew to England to see Rob. Di went a couple of times, I only once. He told us he was 'coming out.' Heck,' I said, 'so what? You're still you.'

We've always seemed close to our two children and I think one factor was that we'd always used our Christian names when talking to them. It wouldn't be 'Go to your mum.' It would be, 'Go to Di.' So they grew up calling us Mike and Di. The grandchildren did too, as they arrived. My reasoning is that they knew the relationship; why not use a name?

Anyway, I wasn't sure what the folks would say about Rob's admission, but they said exactly what I'd said. 'We love you, cos you're you. There aren't conditions.'

Di also went to the U.S., a trip paid for by Henny Maurenbrecher who was our spiritual guru. Her daughter, Noes our friend from the early days, accompanied Di while I remained behind looking after Tess. It took me a number of years before I accepted the spiritual paths Henny talked about.

I clearly remember the night before Di left for the U.S. because we'd organized a moonlight walk across a gas pipe over the Waikato and I was feeling the onset of the malarial sweat and shuddering I've had on and off since I returned from Idris (National service years).

The four feet diameter pipe transferring the Kapuni gas across the Waikato is about two kilometres upstream from the Tuakau Bridge. It was and, as far as I know still is, protected at either end by a 10 m x 10m square of meshed wire surmounted by barbed wire. However a locked gate offered entry, especially as a previous explorer had almost removed the barbed wire above it. I had discovered all this on an earlier reconnaissance expedition when we had been deterred from completing a crossing by the appearance of a car at the far end. A night foray was the answer.

The party comprised Sally and Rob, Alec, not yet Sally's husband, a locum doctor he was training, a couple of friends and myself. Di and another friend were to ferry the canoes across the river to pick us up at the further bank. We scrambled over the gate, putting an old sheepskin over the remains of the barbed wire on top. Then there was a vertical ladder inside a cylinder made up of circular hoops, from which we stepped onto a two foot wide mesh path with the pipe to its immediate left and a handrail to the right. It was nowhere as intrepid as all the precautions implied but it was dark, and unknown. We went, obviously, in single file. The river glinted about thirty feet below us, swirling around the huge blocks of concrete holding up the pillars on which the pipe rested.

Our procession stopped.

'What's up?'

'Gap in the path. Floor's gone.' Pause. 'It's okay, you can jump over.'

One after another we arrived at the gap, about four feet of nothing.

'Be a bit of a splash if you missed your footing,' said Sally.

'More like a splotch,' I amended. 'You'd land on the concrete.

At this stage the locum turned round and muttering about stupid country oafs lacking any imagination or sensitivity walked back the way we'd come. (*En passant*, why isn't the plural of 'oaf' 'oaves'?) Anyway we picked him up later, everyone negotiating the gap without any splashes or splotches.

Back home, I broke out into an enormous sweat. Di offered to remain in N.Z. but Alec gave me a dose of something and three days later I had returned to normal.

I was talking about Launceston before I was side-tracked..... It had a gentle, laid-back ambience, maybe ideal for retirement. There was a large reserve dominated by the gorge which in winter could be a raging tumble of white water and in summer a gentle stream winding its way among the rocks. Peacocks rambled about the park, especially around the cafeteria. Early morning saw Wallabies hopping through the shrubs and in spring there were huge swathes of daffodils which surpassed the spread of yellow Di had achieved in our own section. Di's favourite colour was yellow. Yellow curtains, a yellow front door, a yellow bedspread. And in spring, clumps of daffodils.

Reputed to be the longest single wire contraption of its kind in the southern hemisphere, world, or maybe just Australia, an endless succession of chairs transported visitors from one side of the gorge to the other peering down at the lake of dammed up water funneling out to the sea.

We both enjoyed Lonnie. Josephine and two years later, Sophie were born and spent their early years there. We saw them grow from babies to pre-schoolers. While I recorded Tasmanian life on a DVD camcorder, Di clicked away with a camera, ending up with an enormous collection of albums which I later reduced to manageable proportions. Well, one.

Sally split with Jan during a game of cribbage she and I were playing.

Jan, at door with suitcase and guitar, 'Right, I'm going.'

Sally, 'Hold on. I've got a good hand.'

Jan was an excellent musician, knew how to please. But he was ineffectual, would promise but rarely deliver, didn't enjoy working and was happy to let Sally carry the burden of running the house. Had five kids from previous relationships for whom he was expected to pay maintenance, failing which it would be Sally's responsibility. Yes - ouch!

Ultimately Sally, Jose and Soph moved to Frankston. It certainly made visiting her easier and much as she loved Launceston it certainly kick-started her life again.

Meantime, when not in Australia there were Duke of Edinburgh tramps, and canoeing. I first became involved with the D.O.E. after having a chat with one of the teachers at Tuakau College about the school trips I'd led. I'd explained my philosophy.

Young people don't need expensive trips. One of the major justifications of a school trip is the different perspectives we have of each other when teachers and pupils when in environments other than the classroom. You don't have go to India for that. Canoe down the river, tramp through the bush at Wairamarama, walk up Puke o Tahinga and then out to Limestone Downs. Crawl through the cave at the back of Begg's farm and follow the ridge back to Phillip's woolshed.

'How about you lead some of our kids on Duke of Edinburgh trips?' she asked.

To those unfamiliar with the scheme initiated by the Duke of Edinburgh to encourage self-reliance and goals for the age group 14 – 25, I'll explain briefly. It consisted of three awards, Bronze for the 14-15 year olds, Silver for 16 -17, Gold for the 17 up to 25. Each level consisted of four components. Community Service, a physical activity, a cultural pursuit, an expedition. The Gold award had a fifth component being residential. It is an excellent scheme but I'm uncertain of its present popularity among teenagers.

Keryl persuaded me to take over the expeditions, offering to pay me, something I reluctantly accepted at first as she insisted. I think she wanted to be able to have someone accountable if anything went wrong. Pretty soon however, particularly when the DoE became officially recognised as a part of Tuakau College's out of the classroom curriculum and handed over to a Deputy Principal, I became a volunteer helper. Now, apart from giving each participant an equipment and point of departure and arrival list, (for benefit of parents), I was obliged to fill in innumerable forms. These included a RAMS (Risk and Management Assessment), school policy, and my credentials. I'm sure there was something else, probably an acceptance of total responsibility in the event of disaster.

Somewhere in the previous years in a moment of surprising prescience I'd undertaken an Outdoors Education paper through Massey University and my C+ Certificate was more valuable than all the trips I'd ever led over bygone years. Today most schools employ professional guides leading Expeditions through the Waitakares, Tongariro, Waikaremoana and other wonderful destinations. That's if DoE still operates. I became a convener for DoE at Onewhero Area School for the years 2008 -2012 and this involved registering youngsters and checking their progress. I'd joined up with a fellow local, John Alley, who married Donna of Cinderella fame, and between us we tramped through bush and canoed rivers with hundreds of young ones, from Tuakau and from Onewhero. Later on Bridget joined up and brought a little order into the somewhat slap-dash methods we two males had used.

I'd always had the thought that Donna she and Rob would eventually join up but, hey…All my life I've had heaps to do with the Casey family of which Donna was one of the two girls and two boys. I remember playing with Mike, the younger son and heaps of little ones at the school bus-stop; of Mike once leaning casually against a goal-post when his girl-friend, Francine was playing as goalie, the only girl in our soccer team and the opposition asked who the big guy was; of once belting Tommy, the eldest, because he insisted on going on a cross-country run dressed in his going home clothes and we both knew he was going to stop off at his house on the way past.

'Get changed into P.E gear or…you're for it.'

'Okay, give it to me.'

So I did. Not that I made a habit of physical punishment. My father had never hit me or Derek, my brother. Apart from one moment in a canoe when I smacked Rob across the face and immediately regretted it, I never used physical violence, although Sally has said Di used to threaten her with me. If I did, I can't remember. My heart wasn't in it.

Janine was the other Casey daughter but I had little to do with her, it was Donna I knew best of them all. Over the years since the first time I came across her in the swimming pool and she joined Rob and Sally being tossed from my shoulders, through the days at school, the trips, the drama club, sailing, the music, she's been part of the Onewhero circle Di and I moved in.

Still, John Alley, the feller Donna married instead of Rob, was good value. Together we would preview the areas we proposed taking the various DoE groups on foot since Di and I had navigated most of the streams and rivers.

In the late nineties I'd suggested investing money in a fleet of up to date canoes which we could hire out as another string to our financial well-being. We spent $3000 on two long Canadians, two fast 12 foot Duras and four tubby Minnows. With two two-seat canoes and an extremely tippy flat-bottomed thing I loved giving to know-alls, we had a fleet. Admittedly, I doubt if we recovered our costs but it gave us and many DoE participants heaps of fun.

On one occasion Di and I had been held up by fallen trees while exploring the Mangatawhiri stream. We arrived at Mercer where Dad was to meet us, two hours late. By this time he'd rung the police demanding search parties be organized. I could imagine the conversation.

'My son's missing.'

Policeman, 'Yessir…. How old is your son?'

'He's sixty four.'

'How long has he been missing?'

'Two hours.'

Which reminds me.

We once had a school trip to a small lake on top of a hill near Waikaremoana. Ralf, Tony and a couple of mates consulted a map and decided to bring the canoes we intended to use on the lake, up a stream descending from the lake into the bigger one below. We left them clad merely in shorts, excitedly placing the canoes in the stream and proceeded on foot, ignoring remarks of passersby who felt that carrying sacks of vegetables wasn't ideal. By now you've probably gathered, cheapness was a premium necessity for all my school trips. We budgeted on $5 per person per day. This included something for petrol.

We didn't see Ralf et al for another thirty-six hours by which time we were a bit concerned and spoke to a ranger who had turned up. No cell-phones in those days.

'Give 'em another day,' he told us.

So we did and later they arrived very tired and without canoes. They had gone up the wrong stream, had to sleep out, covering themselves with ferns, then trekked back to the start, dumped the canoes at a ranger's hut and finally arrived exhausted and somewhat peckish at the Waikariti Hut.

'We're just going on a tramp. I don't expect you want to come?'

Before all that carry-on we'd used Ralf's motley collection of fibre class canoes and two two-person wooden canoes. One was nicknamed Simone and was already twenty years old in 1988. We'd also used a double cockpit wooden canoe someone had offered me while we were waiting at a bus-stop in Manurewa. I'd collected that from its owner in Weymouth, and hence the canoe earned the same name.

We also had a large bath-tub of a canoe about eight feet long which was purchased when we realised my home-built dinky (I have not misspelt the word) was too small. This was prior to buying Blossom.

One of the very first canoe trips we ever undertook was from the waterfall at Camp Adair; from the bottom of waterfall I hasten to add, to somewhere near Clevedon. We chose this because the calm waters of the Waikato were not exciting enough. The group assembled: Ralf, Tony, John, Sally then aged seven, Rob aged nine, Di and me.

Sally sat in front of me. The stream was very different from the Waikato. It ran faster around boulders, it frequently slid over minor waterfalls.

The other canoeists had problems with the length of their craft, Sally and I had a different one. With me seated at the rear of the cockpit, and after plunging over a rock into a pool, the rear of our canoe went down. Water flooded in.

We sank. After the sixth or seventh sinking Sally told me she intended swimming down the rest of the way and did so. My daughter still enjoys canoeing which under the circumstances seems surprising.

Over the years, while we're on the subject of canoeing, or kayaking, I've been down the Whanganui three times. The first was a local 'friends and idiots' trip in Dec 1983 assembling with a varied assortment of canoes, a couple of wooden single home-made ones, a couple of Ralf's and an aluminium dinghy John Casey had borrowed from a mate. This carried the gear we couldn't squeeze into the canoes. Apart from John there was his daughter Donna and son Mike, Rob, Sally, Di and me and

Sue who was the first one to capsize at the first of what proved to be over a hundred rapids. Di joined Sue in the river shortly afterwards. I joined John in the tinnie for the first rapid, walking back along the bank after pulling up my canoe on the bank. Apprehensively we entered the rapid, John raising the outboard. We sat, paddles somewhat irresolutely poised, wondering what piece of equipment we should try to salvage first as the current grabbed us and we hurtled through the white water.

It was exhilarating. We found that the boat knew better than we how to navigate the river. It didn't want to hit rocks any more than we did and would whirl around them without much input from the occupants.

We stopped at a couple of huts, we camped on a bank. At a rocky bend in the river I witnessed the tinnie hurtle towards the rocks, Sally in the bows lifted off the seat in mid-stroke her paddle furiously beating the air. Heard John yell, 'Hold on Sally, this is it!' Then a wave crashed into the rock, bounced back and pushed them clear.

Mike tipped in a couple of times and cracked the fibre-glass hull but we bogged it up and carried on.

We were swept past the track to 'The Bridge to Nowhere' but determined to find it another time.

The second time down the Whanganui was with the new canoes. Di and I were in the large Canadian canoe with the gear for four in the middle. A friend, Bridget and her cousin had the minnows, nine foot open bath-tubby things. We decided to start at Taumaranui instead of Pipiriki because it was the first time Di and I had been in white water with the lengthy Canadian and we thought we'd test the calmer waters first. Shortly after we'd set off, we were confronted by a divide in the river; I chose the calmer left hand bit while the others headed for the white stuff.

A hundred metres further on our bit of river ended in a series of concrete steps, the water streaming down them into a whirling mass at the bottom.

'Oh....Lean back.

We bounced down the steps, the bow was pushed down. Di hurled herself backwards and I paddled furiously. In calmer water we discovered we were half full of water, but floating level. That trip we even got to see 'The Bridge to Nowhere' the four of us sitting in the Canadian canoe and crossing over from our campsite on the opposite bank delicately spreading our weight.

The third time was in 2015 when I was helping out with Cubs. We had hired about nine Canadians for the Tuakau Cub and Scout leaders Whanganui expedition. One appeared terribly top-heavy containing not only two large, heavy parents but also an extra hand in the form of a cub seated in the middle on top of a heap of rucksacks. I offered to have some of their gear and the cub. This was all transferred, but they still managed to capsize the canoe regular intervals. In fact at the ultimate rapid they were one of five capsized canoes. The Whanganui was full of upside canoes, swimming figures and floating gear. It would have been an impressive photograph for the Cub magazine but unfortunately my camera was a casualty which I sacrificed swimming out to a couple of people clinging to a canoe drifting past.

Most of our canoeing forays had been on the Waikato and tributaries, along muddied water through paddocks where grazing cows looked up at the novelty. One year, after torrential rain and large ponds of water where before there had been only grass, a group of guys from the Tuakau soccer club whose game had been called off came upon two goats, a mother and kid with water lapping around the belly of the latter. They were standing on what had been the island opposite Pokeno and they'd obviously found a high point. We paddled over. The two large Canadians were held together while I waded across to the poor trembling animals. They remained frozen as I lifted the kid and a couple of us dragged the nanny-goat into a Canadian.

We released them on the bank where they stood still, letting the blood return to their numbed limbs.

'They would have made a good dinner,' said Jock watching the goats walk slowly up the hill.

We ignored him.

Di and I twice came down the Waipa, which meets the Waikato at Hamilton. The first time after we'd stopped off to leave the car, Di had a bout of food poisoning and we had to terminate the trip. I left her and Tess at some guy's house while he and I drove to where we'd left our car. When we returned Tess was standing on the floor in front of the sofa Di was lying on. A large Alsatian was staring somewhat bewildered at the little blonde blob snarling furiously at him.

The second time we descended the Waipa also ended prematurely for Di. We were accompanying Anna and Hayley on their Duke of Edinburgh practice canoe trip for their Gold qualification. Chris and Paul were in one double, Di and I in the other and Hayley and Anna in two singles.

Di and I were arguing; what else? When we encountered a fallen log from which a four foot section had been cut to allow the water to pour through. We were the last canoe to negotiate the gap and what with one thing and another, I misjudged it. The bows hit the log, the canoe swung broadside onto the fast flowing river, tipped, filled with water and then capsized. I somehow stepped briskly onto the log. Di and Tess disappeared underneath the canoe and log.

I saw Di's head bob up. 'Geez'. I breathed a sigh of relief as I saw her start swimming to the bank.

Then I saw Tess struggling in the white water. 'Grab Tess,' I yelled to Paul standing on the bank.

It was ages before I could convince Di that the only reason I'd asked them to help Tess and not her, was that I'd seen her heading ashore.

To complete the incident, a farmer brought two tractors over to haul out the log and recovered the canoe. Every wooden component was broken but the plastic hull was still complete. It was repairable but not useable until the wood was replaced. Di, Tess and Chris went home overland, Paul the two girls and I finished the trip. On a later journey the two girls canoed the Waikato and ultimately received their Duke of Edinburgh Gold award from the Governor General.

Canoe trips from karapiro, or the Narrows or Hamilton down to the Tuakau Bridge became commonplace during the 1990s and first decade of the new millennium, either as school trips or as part of the Duke of Ed award. The stretch between Hamilton and Ngaruawahia is measured in bridges and palatial houses and banks of trees. Once we stopped at the Turangawaiwai marae, spending the previous night on a bank learning our waiata.

That was the school trip where having seen everyone abed, I drifted off to sleep in my tent, being woken by the sound of voices. On investigation I discovered four Maori boys seated around a gas-burner, smoking.

I let rip.

'Stupidity....waste of gas....inconsideration'. I was stopped in mid-flow by an indistinct hollow booming sound. We looked at each other by the light of the gas stove. Beyond these flickering blue flames it was pitch black. The river and where we were standing was one swathe of darkness. The booming noise grew louder and suddenly we saw it- an indefinable shape outlined with a variety of coloured lights. A booming unearthly sound surrounded by stars.

The boys as one, leapt to their feet. 'Ka mate, ka mate'

They stamped their feet, beat their chests, screamed defiance. Shit! Was I glad to have them with me.

And then their voices sagged and we watched the river boat pass and people wave. A midnight excursion.

'Oh, go to bed,' I said to the boys.

Several times we took a mob of people from the Bridge to Frost's landing at night. We'd choose the night of the full moon when it rose about nine o'clock and the silvery glow poured down on the black waters. From the bows of the canoes would spread the gleaming white V's vivid on the still surface like the trail of skis on virgin snow.

Rob has a Minnow and Dura, the sailing club has two Minnows and the rest are in the garage at Onewhero.

Chapter Twenty seven. The Dwen family of Te Kohanga.

When we arrived in Onewhero for the second time Ralf was in the third form and after he left school much of our spare time was spent with him and his mates. He was almost school captain in 1970 but he and his rival contender had an argument about the temperature of the sixth form classroom on the day the position came up for discussion by the staff. The argument resulted in a window falling out of its frame and the third member of Form 6 became school captain.

After leaving school Ralf was for almost twenty years at a loose end. He helped around the farm eventually running it for a few years when his father died. He illustrated bizarre characters for stories, he caught and sold whitebait. He lived in a small hut which had once been the habitat of the manager of a whitebait factory situated next to it. The factory contained rusting machinery and souvenirs of a once flourishing industry – and was perched on the river bank. Behind it a totara covered hill sloped up to a small clearing with kumara pits where in by-gone ages Maoris had stood guard on the river. Opposite an indentation in the land was reputedly the footprint of one of the Gods.

He put together the first fleet of canoes, following up adverts in the paper and rumours of fibre glass canoes that only needed a bit of bog. These were fearfully abrasive on the thighs as they rubbed against the increasingly hairy bits of fibre breaking off from the resin. But he did collect a large open green canoe which accompanied the fleet Di and I eventually bought. The thwart in the middle of this canoe had cracked and the craft sort of snaked through the water rather than glided until Ralf screwed the two section to a piece of wood and stuck a beer-crate under it.

Ralf teamed up with another character who had built a house close to the alleged foot-fall on the other side of the river. Athel always wore an opossum hat with the tail attached, and a woollen swanny trailing over his jeans. A belt with a holstered knife completed the backwoodsman image. Athel parked a car upstream near a place called the Elbow, which was also the local refuse dump, and used a small dinghy to get there. He also had another car cached near Ralf's place. I don't think registration occurred to him.

Over the following years Ralf transformed the tin one-roomed shack he'd started with into a towering edifice sprouting balconies and protruding rooms, each wall alive with multi-coloured glass windows. Inside, a staircase wound its way randomly up to the three floors and into an attic. Small rooms are discovered hidden inside others. Di and I were part of the team that helped insert the original four enormous poles into the holes Ralf had dug. We held the ropes keeping the things vertical while Ralf concreted them into place.

'Building permit?' You're joking. Apart from the natural reaction of the good kiwi bloke to officialdom, the land close to the Waikato river changes, if not at every tide, at least sufficiently often to make surveying at the best problematical. Athel had suffered from this when, failing health compelling a move to warmer climes, he tried to to sell the house he'd built. He couldn't get a title to it because the section didn't exist. It was the insurance payout after a fortuitous fire razed his property that funded his escape to Whangarei.

So many people have stayed at the River house as it became known. In fact Ralf once received a letter from Canada addressed to 'Ralf, River house, Auckland, N.Z.' Di and I have taken relatives and friends there. We've stood on a balcony at night listening to the moreporks; we've watched a large silver moon light the river, felt the infinite peace that living close to nature brings. And if the brrrr of a passing motorboat disturbs the serenity occasionally, well, it's a reminder that the outside world still exists.

Once there was a wooden throne situated at the end of a rickety jetty. On a school trip, overnighting at the house, after a moonlit expedition, we had a desperate moment when our numbers didn't add up until we found someone asleep on the throne. That was the trip where we'd built a large raft and had a fire on a sheet of corrugated iron so we could cook some of Di's famous griddle cake mixture. Somehow Ralf got tipped in and we wouldn't let him climb back on until we suddenly realized things were turning nasty. Not physically nasty, Ralf is too good-natured for violence but he was capable of ripping the raft apart and had made a successful assault on part of it before two of us sacrificed ourselves and joined him in the river.

I keep in contact with the Dwens through Ralf's eldest brother, John whom I first saw, in 1962, delivering a speech for a school competition. It astonished me that he didn't win. Maybe his sense of humour offended the judges. He's reentered my life after forty years. Most days we swap conjectures, philosophical insights and occasional insults over the inter-net. So I keep abreast of Ralf's life. He became a church pastor and periodically flies to India with Sue, his wife, an ex-Onewhero Dental Nurse. There he spreads the gospel while building schools, working with minimalistic materials and tools. I've seen him in the flesh a couple of times, big, a bearded beaming face, glad to see me. At the moment he and Sue have some people in the River house who need 'a bit of peace', to get themselves together again. And there are three young boys requiring a home. He and Sue have kind of adopted them.

Chapter Twenty eight. Powered parachute ZKFLT 1998

A windless summer in 1998 meant a dearth of paragliding days and watching Pete Bovill flying towards Wairamarama seated amongst a heap of struts and translucent wings finally induced me to enter powered flight. At first I considered buying the conventional microlight actually going as far as having some hours instruction in them but no money was committed until I came across a powered parachute dangling from a garage ceiling in Tuakau.

It had been built by someone who, having read a book about them, built what was designated Tidco 101. There never has been a Tidco 102 but I suspect there were a couple of unregistered ones flying. The one I bought, FLT, had collided with power lines. Immediately prior to this the pilot had the fortitude and presence of mind to leap from the machine preferring the 20feet drop beneath him to electrocution. Following this, parental pressure plus, I suppose, a feeling that fate had been tempted to its limits, compelled the pilot to sell the whole outfit for $1500. I took the engine to an ex-pupil who owned the local Rotax franchise who proclaimed it fine, and the canopy to Wind and Waves who removed the burnt portions, checked the lines and returned it ready to go.

So it only left me to find out how to do get it into the air.

I found the designer of Tidco 101 who handed me the instruction manual. This was a succession of three sketches on an A4 sheet stating briefly —a) this was the easiest and safest form of flying, b) get a group of likeminded idiots to share the blame/cost (actually I made that up) and c) How to take off in three easy moves. (i) Lay canopy on ground behind machine. (ii) Open throttle. (iii) Race forward and leave the ground.

From my paragliding experiences I could see the logic in all of this. Still, I had a word with Pete about it first; he advised me to take it easy and do little rabbit hops to get the feel of it. This seemed common-sense and that is how I intended to proceed – none of this gung-ho stuff. Incidentally, Di was consulted about costs, and as she was buying expensive bits jewelry and had started her own side-line in something called Ambotose – heaps more of that later – she let me do my thing too. At this time, what with income from our two home-built (almost) rental properties, plus superannuation plus bits of finance from the occasional bit of relief teaching, and Rob and Sally having left home, our financial situation was a happy one.

On the tenth of March 1998, with a gentle head-wind, I spread the canopy out in the paddock belonging to Dave Bovill, Pete's older brother, who owned the paddock on the other side of our shared boundary fence. I had yet to register my new ownership but felt that a few unofficial flights before I committed myself would go unnoticed. The paddock sloped very gently upwards, about 200m long. Behind me was the road and up ahead a power line but to my right was my section, to the left an ancient fence constructed from concrete posts with a rusty barbed wire cemented into the top. This fence separated the strip from a hill sloping down to the Kaipo Flats. This was ideal because if need be I could swerve over the fence if I was insufficiently high to clear the power line. Not that I intended doing more than bunny-hops, but it was all worth bearing in mind.

I looked around. No-one. I hadn't advertised my intentions. Okay. I should be able to get maybe three hops in before I reached the far fence. I pulled the starting cord. Third pull..... Brrrm. Then into the seat. Harness on. Deep breath. Remember, three hops. Opened the throttle, shot forward and found myself about fifteen feet off the ground. Ah well. Yep, I'd easy clear the power line... Wouldn't need to veer anywhere. Heck, I was flying!. This was so different from paragliding....I had an engine. I could point myself in any direction.

I made a shakey circuit of the Kaipo Flats and was then presented with the problem of landing. Come to think of it, my manual hadn't covered the return to earth. Obviously must jiggled the throttle. I jiggled and possibly juggled. The end fence got closer. Shit. Still two feet off the ground I switched the engine off and landed, or to be more accurately fell two feet onto the ground.

I disassembled myself and found I'd badly bent the axle and Pete who'd watched the whole enterprise from his tractor down in the Kaipo Flats arrived to point out two broken struts.

But what the hell. I'd flown!

A couple of weeks later with a straightened axle and welded struts I was in the air again determined to circumnavigate the Kaipo Flats and conclude with a gracious, or at least undamaged, landing. I reached the cemetery, where generations of Onewhero pioneers rest and while philosophically peering down, a distinct drop in the volume of engine noise led me to suspect a malfunction of one cylinder. While debating an emergency landing at Pete's strip the decision was taken from me. When only the sound of the whistling wind remained even I could determine that the engine had given up completely. Again a bent axle but now, added to the problem, a defunct engine.

Before the purchase of a new engine in 2012, every flight started with a question mark over it- would the engine fire? Apart from that there was my own ignorance of flying a powered machine, being unable to assess its tolerance to wind without experiment and still not a hundred percent certain I was rigging it correctly. But the years passed and I learnt.

Di was complimented on her ability to watch me leave the house not knowing what might return.

An interesting example occurred while preparing for a party one afternoon.

'Right, Di. Is there anything else for me to do?' I'd vacuumed, tidied, was hanging around.

'Not really.'

'Might go for a short flight.' All my flights were short.

'Don't do anything stupid. I need help here.'

'I'll stay if you want.'

'Oh go.'

During an earlier aborted take-off – to be strictly truthful, I hadn't aborted the flight, the machine had – I half rose and then completed a landing roll having inadvertently put the four wires connecting canopy to machine on backwards. Surprisingly the damage, inflicted at a fairly slow speed, was negligible consisting of a broken tube which fitted over one of the aforementioned wires, keeping them upright. I hadn't got round to replacing the broken one but decided if I made a good take-off it would stay vertical by force of the wind.

I was wrong. Having taken-off, the machine made a sharp turn to the left. It continued to do this as I was blown briskly across the landscape in what from the ground must have seen gracious circles. Under the circumstances, a credible landing was made on top of Tilsey's hill and a Tilsey family member helped me push the machine to the gateway on the main Wairamarama Road.

With reluctance I rang Di requesting humbly she drive the Ute to pick up me and the machine.

The reply was terse. A few minutes later the Ute shot past me and disappeared round a bend. A quarter of an hour later another car arrived containing Di and Chris Walters.

Put briefly Di, driving Newton, the Ute, had reached Twin Bridges, at the bottom of a hill about two kilometres from where I was waiting. Realizing her mistake and by now in an unwholesome state of mind, she had raced back up the hill and failed to negotiate the bend at the top fortuitously choosing a pliable bit of gorse to park the Ute in.

After listening to this account I found a comment difficult. 'Ah,' I replied. Then lightly, after all, she was okay, that was obvious. 'Much damage to the ute?'

This was the wrong thing to say.

'And what about me, chasing all over the countryside after you? What about asking how I am?'

I can't recollect much of that party.

My learning curve was long but, due to guardian angels and luck I survived it There were the inherent safety features of the machine which couldn't exceed 20 mph, and above all had a built-in parachute which together meant I am here today.

Pete commented that I'd experienced most of those events on fixed wing craft. Bearing in mind that I am writing in 2018, 20 years after my inaugural flight, here are some of the highs and lows.

The first flight over the Waikato to Aka-Aka had me glowing with some of the success Christopher Columbus must have experienced when he landed on the American coast. Then came the day I circled Pukekohe hill. That was tremendous.

Once, in those early days, while flying over the Maurenbrecher house, the throttle fell off. I think this must be a unique occurrence. Only Henny remained in the house, Ton dying a few years previously and the family having left home. I had flown low and seen her wave. Cheerily I waved back before shoving the throttle forward and hearing the engine roar, the ground start diminishing and a sick feeling in my stomach as the throttle lever snapped off and acted according to Newton's gravitational law.

Maybe there were other options but with the engine howling at full throttle I could only think about hitting forbidden heights. So I looked around, saw a reachable paddock (I missed it), and switched off the engine. Blissful silence, a few touches to align another spot, a few more touches to miss a cow trough and then not a bad landing at all. A friendly farmer helped me move to a more convenient paddock and in a couple of weeks I was again airborne. With a stronger throttle lever.

There were the summer mornings with perfect take-offs, and flights over the hills of Wairamarama or the day I landed on Karioitahi beach, refilled from petrol Di brought along in the Ute and then flew back; being one of the big boys with his toy at the Aka-Aka school fete; touring the roads of Onewhero, taking photographs of houses and then knocking on doors to sell them at $20 each to the enormous irritation of the aerial–photographers who tried to sell their own product in the district.

And memorable events still happened.

Corri and Zettie, his wife, arrived in Onewhero in 2003. He is an aeronautical engineer and then had a job at Auckland airport. Pete had invited him down to investigate the strip and as I was there, they stopped to witness one of the most horrible take-offs I ever performed. A cross-wind took me sideways and rather than abort the T/O I reckoned I could get over the hedge to my left. When it became obvious that I couldn't, I flew into it, fortunately cutting the engine first.

Corrie took a great interest in the powered parachute, eventually substituting two main rigging lines instead of four and completely changing the landing gear. Now the axle has been replaced by suspension on either wheel. Prior to this Neill Webster the aluminium welder in Pukekohe had refused to repair the machine again unless I changed the material used in the chassis to chrome- molly which he'd done free of labour costs. My guardian angels. Okay, they're funny sort of guardian angels but...well, later.

Another incident involving a fence rather than a hedge was a bit more serious. Outside my section in Onewhero is the lengthy paddock, the one that had seen my very first take-off. I spread the canopy out at the top end and, while checking the canopy connections, noticed the wind had changed so I would be taking off downwind. Thereupon I disconnected things and transported the lot to the other end of the paddock meaning there would be a slight uphill take-off. Just before settling myself into the seat, the wind rippled the canopy....behind me. 'Bother.' Or words to that effect.

Still if the wind was that fickle I could spend the morning moving up and down the paddock. 'Sod it.'

I shoved the throttle forward and meandered up the hill. One thing was certain. We wouldn't rise over the power lines. I veered to the left and almost cleared the fence, the wheels just clipping the top strand of wire. This tipped the whole machine forwards. I was still flying but....There was a hedge on my right but if I flew into that with my momentum....I had a momentary vision of bowling head over heels down the slope.

Instead of which we slid to a gentle stop half way down the hill, the machine graciously braking itself with a turn into wind. Funny though; I was leaning over to the left. Removing myself from what could have been a heap of tangled aluminium struts, I saw the only damage inflicted by the incident. The left wheel had detached itself in the process of separating the top strand of the fence from the concrete posts. The axle stud had providentially braked the downhill landing.

Pete, who as usual, had observed the whole scene from the seat of a tractor in the Kaipo Flats arrived and, with a bit of corrugated iron discovered in Dave's rubbish dump as substitute for a wheel, I was dragged back home. The foreman at the engineering works in Tuakau made me an axle stud which is now the strongest part on the machine, Dave replaced the concrete posts with wooden ones explaining that I had merely advanced a job that had been hovering on necessity for some time. And we were ready for the next adventure.

Actually the worst thing of all didn't happen to me but to another powered parachute which was using Pete's strip. The pilot had bought a super-de-luxe model after witnessing it on-line. It was powered by a 90horse engine and was basically a silvered pod capable of carrying two people and a pile of luggage. The most awe inspiring feature was the dashboard which measured every conceivable thing imaginable from airspeed (unnecessary, a powered parachute has only one speed, opening the throttle will make you go up, and closing it makes you go down), humidity, time lapse, variation in height the possibility of returning safely. I made that up. The pilot ultimately went solo, but both Pete and I had reservations about the machine and the pilot. He was instructed by the guy who had grounded me because my roundie parachute was obsolescent, back in the days. He was right. Landings had been getting harder. (Not more difficult just more of a bang). Steering was problematic. Still…. The sod had grounded me.

John test-piloted Neil's machine one morning and he did a circuit fairly quickly, testing the sensitivity of the canopy by zig-zagging across the sky. I complimented him on his thoroughness.

'Couldn't keep the bloody thing straight,' he answered.

They adjusted this and that. Privately I thought the canopy and machine lacked compatibility. The machine, resembled a space-age assemblage of unnecessary grandeur held up by a by-gone simplicity. I once flew my faithful Foxtrot Echo Tango alongside – well, to be honest we were separated by at least 100 metres – Neil and his machine out to the Wairamarama hills where I took photographs of him flying his expensive new toy.

It was fortunate I did. A week later, flying just before midday when the wind had started to blow and his son was watching he managed to stall coming into land from a sharp right hand turn and sploshed down in Pete's septic pond. This cushioned what could have proved a fatal return to earth. The machine apart from the engine which would need a bit of a clean, was a right-off. Neil escaped with a couple of bones broken in his face and a real life experience.

I sent him some photographs of his machine, proud and gleaming in the sunlight over the rolling landscape of Wairamarama.

I continued my flying, making DVDs of the various roads and houses I flew over. Peter Taylor's wife put out a large blue sheet so I wouldn't film the wrong cottage. I followed the railway lines from Noes' house in Patumahoe to Weck's air-strip in Glenbrook feeling that I had joined the ranks of the aerial pioneers who had used the same navigational method. Rob took a DVD of me taking off and while I was gone used up most of what was left of the battery trying to make the life-story of a cow interesting.

Pete and I decided to be the first people in Onewhero to see the start of the new millennium. We planned our take-offs for six o'clock. However, neither flying vehicle could be persuaded to co-operate, and despite us sweating blood the engines refused to start.

We repeated the process the following day, successfully, but it didn't seem as significant. This is one of those happenings which typify the sort of flying we do. These days most microlite flying closely resembles general aviation. You press buttons and things function as expected. The older microlite pilot is always gratified and vaguely surprised to land at the same strip without experiencing some unnerving event.

The group of us, Pete and Dave Bovill, Corrie, me, didn't ask for fast machines capable of flying long distances, navigated by a moving map. We liked the idea of something slow, not necessarily going anywhere, just being part of the sky for half an hour, getting our perspectives right as we saw the world from 2000feet – real enough to know we belonged to it but, as we saw the misty blue horizons merging into the far-off sea, sufficiently distant to appreciate the oneness of it all.

Okay, that'll wrap up flying for a bit. From the early days of parachuting, through paragliding and powered parachuting, flying has been part of my life. It was Di's for six years too but although offered the chance, after she gave up her private pilot's license the only planes she flew in were the big jets flying her across the Tasman to our daughter and granddaughters.

Heaps of other activities filled in our weeks, but another constant was the monthly visit to the Maurenbrecher house where Keith and Marilyn Masemann, Di, Ton and Noes met to... heck, worship s rather a heavy word.... Well, express gratitude for the shit-hot world we've got. I didn't join immediately but

Henny and Di convinced me that no-one was going to insist I learnt a doctrine or had to conform.

'Take from it what you want, Mike,' Henny said. 'There are many scenes from the many windows of a large house. Some people choose only one window and see only one view; some prefer to draw the all the blinds. What is life, and death about? I can tell you what I think.'

So I became a member of 'The Bridge to Spiritual Freedom.' I don't know whether it still exists but I've geared my understanding of what this life is all about on most of its teachings. But if you're interested, look it up for yourself, read about Mrs Blavatsky. Get a copy of the Urantia Book. I've put together the following hogwash of thoughts. Remember they're as relevant or irrelevant as anyone's. A new chapter is called for.

Chapter Twenty nine. The meaning of life!

Sometime ago I wrote an (unpublished) offering to the Bay of Plenty Times giving advice on the wisdom of making four preparations for retirement – economic security, physical activity, mental stimulus and a philosophy that gives some sort of meaning to life. Get these organized so that they form a basis for a pleasurable retirement. It's no use waiting until you've left work to suddenly appreciate that there's nothing left to do and no reason for doing it. Or not. Anyway. What follows is the odds and ends which make me feel the whole thing wasn't/isn't just a joke. And in any case, if it was/is, then I've had a good laugh on the way.

That's the first point. Nobody, whatever they say, knows about God or an after-life, or why we're here. They might believe and they might make a fortune out of spreading their beliefs, causing heaps of trouble on the way, but they don't know. So – decide on a theory and as long as it's socially acceptable, it's as good as anything else.

We humans are gregarious beings. We need each other. We have common needs. Here's a few but you can make your own list. Air, water, food, shelter, help when we're in strife, hot running water, tertiary education, a gardener, honest political leaders.... Admittedly it's possible to get carried away at this point. Still, seeing that most of these things are shared out reasonably equably is a philosophy all by itself. And it's god enough! And although that was a typo, I'll let it stay. There can be more though.

Firstly, I presume there is an after-life. Let's face it, if there isn't we won't know. Secondly, there is an Absolute Power that has evolved. It is Totality. It does not know us as individuals but just as we are unaware of the millions (?) of cells which comprise our existence but without which we cannot function this Totality needs us. There is a layer between us and the Totality which has sought, not always successfully, to explain what the Totality is. I'm not going to try to explain. My advice is, don't listen to anyone on Earth who tries.

However, we have our own direct link to the Totality. We do not need a mediator. Our earthly form comprises four parts. Henny used the analogy of four horses dragging a carriage and although I don't like analogies I'll use it. The horses are: the Physical body which needs exercise, the Emotional body which expresses our feelings, which gives us compassion, love, fear, hatred.

Thirdly, there's the Mental body which processes what the body experiences and works out strategies for life. Lastly there is the Etheric body which I explain as the instincts and characteristics that are in our genes, given us by the millions of ancestors we've inherited them from. (This could be a place to bring in re-incarnation but not yet). And who drives this coach, keeping these four horses under control so none of them ruins the equilibrium? The Mind.

And then the ultimate question, who controls the Mind? What tells you, 'Don't let your mind wander; relax your mind.'

And that is your spiritual connection to the Totality. And what does the Totality want? That's a biggy but here goes.

The Totality wants us to be happy because if we're happy, the Totality is happy.

That's my belief. Someone told me there's a country where happiness is written into the constitution. Hell, doesn't the U.S.A. have something like that? And they've ended up with President Trump!

What the hell, just enjoy the ride and do your best to help others do the same.

I've stuck the daily mediation messages at the end of this bit of my autobiography. You'll find heaps of names of Angels, Elohims , Masters….truly, names don't matter . Don't get hung up on them. I think having some guardian angels you can chat with are important. I've got four and I ask them to keep me alert on the roads, to help me follow my conscience. Yeah, and I know what you're thinking but try it. Give yourself a Guardian Angel – or two, possibly four is greedy- and chat things over with them.

Maybe the Masters referred to are the layer between us and the Totality. Or maybe not. We'll find out, or not. Will we return to sort ourselves out? Don't worry, just have fun. And don't stop others enjoying the ride.

Chapter Thirty. 2000 - 2010
The final years with Di

With Rob and Sally off to learn their own lessons, the world decided to shovel an awful lot of problems into the spaces they'd left. Or rather, we wallowed into them unwittingly, wading into a morass of self-imposed responsibilities and time-consuming activities while overlooking the basics of relaxation and prioritization. No wonder my first inclination was to sub-head this period as the one of illness, pain and death. But that's too negative. Birth balances Death. We accepted the contract when we were born. And those hectic moments... surely they were better than stagnation. Comes back to moderation and I just have the feeling, in that last decade of Di's life, we didn't get the balance right.

631 Te Kohanga Rd is almost on the corner of a right angled bend. Years before, when it had yet to be tar-sealed, I'd heard a bang and discovered a car upside down in a ditch. The driver emerged unharmed and I turned off the ignition.

'Have a cup of tea.

'Ta. I'll use yer phone. Gotta git the tractor.'

People have always popped in. We're a convenient place coming from or going to, town. And there was always tea or coffee available. And we knew so many people... Musicians, ex-pupils, dog-owners who knew their pets were as welcome as they were, kids who wanted to play with the box of cars under the settee. And, come to think of it, animals who just popped in because they wanted company.

The turnover of people living in Rick and Lorraine's house included a couple whose pair of dogs were small enough to scramble through the cat flap. Our first encounter was during a thunder storm when a long-haired Pekinese leapt on the table at which we were seated and desperately licked our faces. A less demonstrative sort of cross between terrier and dachshund looked up at us from the floor. 'They're afraid of lightning,' explained their owner later.

The next couple owned a small kuni-kuni pig called Rosie. During the two years they occupied Rick's old place Rosie and their dog, Flynn became frequent visitors. Rosie discovered the shelves of flour and sugar under the bar and I had to build an extra partition to the front entrance, as she found the customary door too easy to nudge open. In those days it was never locked. Visitors would just shove it open and if we weren't in would shove off out again.

By this time, in 2003, we'd collected Tosswell, a male Labrador Rick had left with a farmer friend when he and Lorraine had moved into Pukekohe. Toss, didn't enjoy life on the farm. It seemed he was treated as a working dog, living outside in a cold kennel and fed minimally - a wholesome and healthy existence but one without the comforts of a family home. He turned up on the doorstep one morning while Di was visiting Sally. By the time Di returned Toss had moved in. I would take Toss and Flynn on walks around the Kaipo Flats where they'd explore the undergrowth alongside the road and sometimes finding an opossum they'd, horribly, kill, or a hedgehog which would merely roll up and defy them.

Toss was the last dog we called our own. I still find it difficult to talk about the dogs I've known, and loved, and seen die.

I wrote the following when Mash died back in 1987:

MASH
Part of my growing up in New Zealand.
Mash, my dog, a large part of my children's youth,
On every outing, town, sea, the bush,
Climbing the Pinnacles,
slogging down the Wainora,
Scrambling over the rocks n limestone caves,
And going mad with rolled up paper
in a chase around the bar.
I remember: you clinging to a surfboard at Ponui
and days of sunshine watching
As I painted or hammered, or dug.
Gentle, loving old dog
with warm brown eyes, following
Following.
God speed, old lady.
May the elementals take good care of you.

I've always written poetry. It's a succinct way of expressing ideas and emotions without having to worry too much about structure or a story line. There's a green book if you're interested with poems going back to the 70's although I can remember writing something that ended up in the School magazine about a china statue Mum had and which Di gave to the Salvation Army and I made her retrieve.

Included in this green book is something Di wrote about Tess:

TESS written by Di 5 Jan 2001

The way I cleaned her eyes every morning,
and she licked the bits.
The way she'd tear at a towel
and growl as I dried her.
The way she followed the little kids round
for biscuits.
The rug on the settee to keep her grease from it
and wrap her up on cold days
Snuggling into bed under the clothes
on very cold nights.
Having my face and ears washed.

So much love, so much love without judgement –
absolutely unconditional.
Water at Henny's.
Always under the keyboard when I played it,
I warmed my feet.

Near me when I went anywhere strange,
and always coming to the toilet with me
in a strange house.
Looking around with a smile
and tail wagging to be lifted up a slope.
Saying 'feet' so that she would
put her feet up to be lifted into the ute.
Head on my leg or lap
and me stroking ears and nose,
Sitting on my lap to see out of the ute,

Lying in the study
to catch the breeze from four doors,
Woofing too late as people came in,
Telling her girl dogs can do anything
and calling her Bat (Batgirl)
The sigh of happiness as she lay down.
Darling Wiss. Miss you so much.

Everywhere I look, there's you –
In the Ute, towel, lead, drinking bowl, water
bottles,
Coming down the road barking
going to Henny's – the greeting
As I come home from shopping,
burying herself in my skirt and me kissing her back,
Coming down first thing in the morning,
'Hello Bat.' And the head lifts
And the tail wags. Defending me
when I'm asleep in the Ute

244

Or ill on the settee that time.
Hearing her puff and the nails click
as she climbed the stairs.
Counting 1 – 6, 1 – 8
as she went down in the night
having asked for the light to be on.

Saying, 'Come and give me a big kiss,'
after I'd combed her (flizzed her).
'Who is the bestest dog?'
as I nuzzle into her stomach and kiss it.
'OK Ding, I'm just going to the garage, the folks.
Do you want to come?'

Body all aquiver, ears pricked, tail wagging.
Asking for something
when I come home from shopping
and moaning at Henny's for us to go home
So she can have her dinner.

All the trunks and steps at the end of the beds
so she can jump up and the oof sound as she did it.
The way she ignored hooch.
My darling girl.
My baby. My friend who chose me,
whose fur was my sanctuary.
My companion who gave so much love.
Being with us everywhere, always.
Dear little silky-furred friend,
we really loved you so much, so very much.

May the Devas watch over you.

(I'm sorry, Di, the last three lines were from the poem I wrote.)

As written earlier, my folks died in this decade, Dad in 2003, Mum four years later. Prior to that they'd had the usual problems associated with ageing, not that Di and I had been immune ourselves since.

Dad had an eye operation. On discharge he persuaded the nurses that he was being picked up, but had them fooled and was on the way to what he thought would be a bus home. But he ended up in the opposite direction. Some business men saw him wandering about in Mangere and gave him a lift back to Manukau from where a member of the clinic admin staff rang us.

His other exploits before the ultimate prank included mislaying his car, the VW they'd brought over from England almost forty years previously and then concluding it must have been stolen. Fortunately some friends from the Senior Citizen club to which they belonged discovered it parked where Dad had left it, in a remote corner of the landscape. He failed his age-required driving test and for the last two years of his life Di or I took them shopping, to their favourite holiday destination in Whitianga, or down to the Port for a stroll on the sand. I'd pop down every Thursday for a game of cribbage with Dad and an instalment of a 'Dad Army'.

Then I stupidly asked him if he'd drive the VW back from outside the Tuakau Hall where there was a Senior Citz meeting. Di and I were going on to Pukekohe and we'd drop them off, Di driving our car, me theirs. Two hours later Jonti knocked on our door. 'Not to worry, your Dad's been in an accident. Your mum's in hospital but is okay.'

He'd taken a corner too wide, hit a car and then bounced into another one. The VW was a write-off. The police were very understanding. I think the sergeant had aged parents of his own. Dad not being licensed, the insurance wasn't interested and paying for the two cars cleared out most of their savings.

All of this is part of the stress of those years. Mum and Di had never been the best of mates. I think Mum felt sorry for Lesley, Di thought she was jealous of the University education she had. Sally took Di's side and both before and after Dad died, whenever the opportunity arose, Sally would do her best to retaliate for what she considered she'd suffered as a girl. For instance, on a visit to New Zealand she would refuse to see them. So mainly Di and I would go over to Australia.

These over the ditch meetings were also fraught with angst. Sally's relationships came and went. Alec, a doctor both medically and by title, left her alone for long periods to further professional advancement. He was dumped after seven years. Jan was a musician who played bass, had five children from three previous liaisons and used Sally as a prop. She had two girls by him, Josephine who was born in 1998 and Sophie who arrived nineteen days into the new millennium. He left while Sally and I were playing crib.

To some extent we were one of the stable elements in the girls' childhood. Obviously Sally was the main one, having to raise them and also provide a sound financial security. We'd cross over twice a year and I'd play Barbie dolls with them, Di would take them shopping, I taught them to go the wrong way up moving elevators, we had tea parties, played on the slide in the park, pushed prams around the Launceston Gorge or sat on the light railway track in Edendale market or we would watch the monkeys in the park and stop Sophie picking coins out of the fountain.

It always felt as if we were walking a fine edge with Sally. Either one of us, more often me, could make a remark that would end in outrage that we could only sit back and take. So we took it.

Meanwhile in Onewhero the years were full-on with Drama club activities – trying to build a youth base by organizing talent quests for various age groups, producing pantomimes with twenty or so young ones ranging in ages of 8 to 16, raising the idea of a Winter Fest of Music and Dance. This later morphed into a Matariki open night mic. Both Di and I were prominent in anything musical. By 2006 the Irish group had almost dissolved; but Pete, Corrie. Donna, nee Casey, Di and formed a group called Hangar Torque.

We actually produced a disk entitled 'Blue Skies Dreaming' which included about ten songs Di and I had written and the group had tweaked. Dori would appear during the week and play songs she'd composed for her own group. And Aiden would pop in to play his fiddle, Charles would bring a guitar and his own quirky songs. And then there was Richard.

I first met Richard Solomons at a gathering of students assembled in a local farmer's house to demonstrate their prowess on the guitar to various mums and dad. It was organized by the tutor. Amongst the younger musicians was a curly-haired middle-aged guy I recognised as being the Bridge-whizz for the local paper, contributing a weekly column outlining the various esoteric calls experts could make given certain cards.

'Wow,' I whispered to Di,' I bet he's good.'

When I encountered him next it was at an inaugural meeting of a group destined to call itself 'Over the Hill' a reference to age combined with location, we all being centred on Onewhero. After attending folk festivals at Auckland Anniversary weekends since the late 1970s and purchasing the quintessential document 'Begged Borrowed and Stolen' Di and I settled on Irish music as a special genre. This has rubbed off on both Rob and Sally, the latter especially.

At one festival, an eight year old Sally met up with an Irish fiddler and in two days had displayed a phenomenal ability on the violin, so great in fact that one of the session musicians raced off to collect a black fiddle which he said needed a good home. Be that as it may, By the millennium's arrival there was a local group attracted by the sound and rhythm of Celtic music. We'd picked up Mandy who played a recorder, Aiden who played a fiddle and Donna who was an ex-pupil who'd been in the same class as Rob. She played guitar. Mandy told us of a newcomer with a real Irish accent who could sing real

Irish songs called Kath Solomons. who was married to Richard.

We all met at our place. Where else? And the Irish Band of Onewhero was launched. Over the years membership has waxed and waned but the only two who've valiantly kept 'Over the Hill' alive have been Richard and I. It even survived my move to Tauranga so that for almost twenty years we've met twice a month at a variety of venues.

We first discovered our similar musical disabilities at Pauanui when we met at Aiden's house for a weekend of music. No-one wanted us to play melody, that being the province of fiddle and whistle so in a lull we mooched off to serenade each other taking it in turns to be the melody instrument picking out the tune laboriously on guitar or mandolin while the other thumped out chords. It was during one of these sessions that Richard made a confession.

'You remember that mini concert thing at Passau's place?'

'Yes, you played a couple of tunes there.

'After that my music teacher said she couldn't teach me anything else.'

'Oh.'

'She fired me.'

I commiserated, remembering being rejected by the Welsh principal and the many times I'd been heavily censured by Di or Rob or Sally because I skipped a few beats to get to a note or hesitated at a critical point. Over the years Richard and I have developed our own style, hanging on to a chord while the other slowed down at a particularly difficult succession of notes, treating errors as an experience to be enjoyed with mild humour. Anyone familiar with Irish tunes will know they are almost always split into two or three sections, each one played twice before shifting on to the following one. We had the practice of playing each song through twice and it was easy to forget which bit you were playing and how many times you'd played it.

'Was that the second time?'

To which the answer would be, 'Yes,' irrespective of the truth.

We take it in turns to choose a tune. Although it probably happened more often, at least twice we've spent ten minutes Richard strumming tune 'X' while I picked tune 'Y', and then repeated the process with the roles reversed and only at the conclusion discovering what had happened, each feeling the other was a bit off but not really enough to mention.

When Zettie and Corrie arrived in Onewhero in 2004 a new life force hit the district both musically and aeronautically. An overweight Zettie organized a fitness group to meet in the Onewhero gym, situated under the pavilion and the property of the Rugby club. I can remember there were about five of us determined to lose weight. Donna, the guitarist, Marieta, a friend of Zettie, Joesy who knew how to operate the equipment so it didn't pull us apart or crush us, Zettie and me. This dwindled within weeks to just Donna and me. We discovered the fee for using gym equipment also permitted us to use the squash courts. She introduced me to squash and this cropped up in conversation with Richard who thereupon challenged me to a game.

So for the next three years until the gym membership fee doubled, Richard and I would meet at the gym, play two games of squash and then go to my house, play our version of music, have a cup of coffee and eat cake. We followed the last three parts of that routine for many years, sometimes in our own homes, seated beside the Hamilton lake, or in the Te Aroha Bridge club rooms. This last is halfway between my home in Tauranga and his back in Onewhero.

We once had a reward system for the winner of the squash games. If I lost we played a revoltingly repetitive tune entitled 'Kid on the Mountain' which I came to loath deeply, not only from its intrinsic faults but because it underlined my deficiencies in squash.

I couldn't find one he really disliked but on the other hand I wouldn't have had many opportunities to inflict it on him. But by God I made him work for the 'Kid' and the occasion he had a sore back I thrashed him.

The whole point of that sprawling drivel is to emphasise how varied interests were during those last ten years of Di's life. She would make the cake Richard demolished, she would sit listening and sighing to our musical efforts, she would pop round to see Zettie, or Zettie would come round to us to discuss the Young People's talent quest or the music for the next play the drama club was putting on.

When the Irish Band dissolved Pete, Donna, Di, Corrie and I formed 'Hangar Torque' a group bonded by aviation playing tunes about flying. Corrie was given the set of drums we'd bought which was, to be honest, a bit of the reason 'Over the Hill' broke up. Di wanted to have a percussion element in the Irish band and Mandy felt this would maker Kath, who played the boron, redundant. I could see both points of view, a perspective which usually offends everybody.

Actually, we all sort of drifted our separate ways. Corrie ended up playing the drums for Hangar Torque, his background as an aeronautical engineer probably accounting for his sense of rhythm. Nobody seemed upset. We made a disk of songs associated with flying through endless blue skies, sunny dreams and burbling engines. Then we got fed up with singing about it and Hangar Torque dissolved.

Only Richard and I, like the occupant of the 'Irish Rover' remain.

My flying throughout this period remained focused on Onewhero. Occasionally I flew around Pukekohe hill managing to meet a man who owned most of it and whose major quandary was how to divide it up amongst his heirs. He eventually walked me over choice areas and I photographed them assembling them into a video which presumably settled his problem.

There are a few DVDs knocking around entitled 'Onewhero Roads' which portray from ground views taken precariously from a moving car with me positioned outside the vehicle with my feet clinging to a strap and my backside on the window frame. Less dangerous pictures were taken from the air.

My proudest, and most financially rewarding video was when Albert Alferinck of Mercer cheese fame hired my skill, (coughs modestly) to make a documentary following the process of changing the milk of Bryce Costar's cows into hunks of gold-medal winning cheese.

What with photography, coaching girls' soccer teams, Duke of Edinburgh tramps and canoeing expeditions, and fixing the machine after bits detached themselves or the engine either wouldn't start or, unpleasantly, stopped in mid- flight. This actually only happened twice, and didn't result in much that couldn't be bent straight again. Apart from these cultural activities, home-life needed to go on. Mowing the section, burning the rubbish, fixing walls and painting. In between we made twice yearly visits to Australia resuming our relationships with our daughter and two grand-daughters. Sally's romances followed a stuttering course, once leaving her in such a depressed state that Josephine and Sophie ended up with us for four months.

To say the first ten years of the new millennium were fairly busy is a colossal understatement. With hindsight, I guess it's reasonable to say we overdid it and to some extent our health suffered. Both Di and I grappling with the physical deterioration of age. She had a knee replacement, I had a stent. Her cholesterol levels needed balancing and she was put on Warfin. This involved lots of blood tests which eventually became so painful she decided to forego them. After all, she had discovered Ambrotose.

Di and I were visiting Sally, and had met up with people who were making a living, almost, by promoting and selling a magic potion called Ambrotose, presumably based on the Ambrosia served to the Gods. Instead of flogging it through pharmaceutical outlets a hierarchical pyramid system had been set up. People were recruited into sets of six and each member of that set recruited a similar number. Everyone paid a commission on any sale made to the person higher up the pyramid.

The higher up the chain....well, you get the picture. From the start I was sceptic. Di believed she had discovered a source of revenue which would solve what she was desperately seeking. She envied the money I made from selling aerial photos, and the insignificant royalties from books. So she sought out customers and hopefully a stack of people beneath her to provide a slice of their own earnings in the scheme.

Not so long down this track, after a biopsy involving a gun fired up my arse extracting bits of prostate I was diagnosed with prostate cancer. There was no argument about this; cancerous cells had been detected. The question was, what to do? We decided on a course of 'Watchful-waiting'.

'In the meantime,' said Di, 'You take three teaspoonfuls of Ambrotose twice a day.'

To cut a long story short, I did and when six months later I had another biopsy to see how the cancer was progressing, there were no cancer cells; anywhere.

So I was convinced Ambrotose contained something and I joined Di's campaign. We preached the benefits of Ambrotose at Lion's Clubs, Rotary, the Heart/stroke club and Women's Federation.

I sang cockney songs; we played a variety of instruments between us: keyboard, guitar, recorder, clarinet and mandolin. I would show a video and give a short talk on my flying experiences, and finally Di would give her spiel on Ambrotose which I would corroborate from my own experience.

The preparation engendered by these presentations over those few months, were the closest I'd been to Di for a very long time. We bought a DVD player and during the evenings we'd settle down to learn new songs and to think of other corporations to approach.

Di decided then that the Warfarin injection she had had every fortnight was too painful. Ambrotose would take care of the problem. She died three months later.

Chapter Thirty one. 25 April 2010. Farewell to Di

We'd intended having our first family re-union in New Zealand after years of us all living in different countries. Admittedly we'd all met up in Frankston, Australia a few years previously, but this April Rob would be bringing over his partner, Wayne, and Sally had the three girls. Daryl had permitted Bonnie to leave the country.

ANZAC day, and the following, were full on. Di, Josephine and Sophie had done the shops, possibly not the 'Di Day' which occurred on the final day of a visit by us to Australia when spare cash was poured out according to anyone's whims, despite the expense.

Here's an example of a Di Day: Josephine, an eight year old, persuaded me to buy, as a Di-Day present. It was a $18 toy kitten which purred when cuddled. At the checkout I discovered I'd read the wrong shelf and the kitten was $70. Four years later when they left Frankston for Melbourne you can guess what got handed in to the Sallies.

But this one ended differently. We had arrived home in Onewhero for dinner, Rob and Wayne were due later the following day. Sally, Di and I sat in the lounge-kitchen while the girls watched television in the bedroom. I read a book.

Suddenly, 'I feel funny, Sally.' And Di slipped from her chair onto the floor.

Sally screamed, ran over and looked at Di and felt her pulse.

I remembered the words of Dori after Dad's collapse. 'Don't hesitate to call for help.' First I checked with Di. She had a pulse but her colour was wrong. Raced to the phone. It was a landline, we didn't have a cellphone. Dialled 999. 'Ambulance.' Gave an address.

'What's wrong?'

'I need help. My wife's unconscious.'

'Is she breathing?'

I looked at Sally. 'No.'

'Is there a pulse?'

I gave up at this stage. 'I need help.'

Rang off, then dialed Di Morris who was in the Fire Brigade and lived close. Asked her to come quickly. She was there in five minutes while Sally and I knelt by Di, breathing into her mouth, numbed by the suddenness of it all.

Di Morris gave CPR until there was a knock on the door. The Onewhero Fire Brigade arrived followed shortly afterwards by St John's with their electric shock machine.

Twenty minutes later. 'We're losing her.'

And finally. 'She's gone.'

A doctor came; then two policemen who asked me to wait outside while they conferred. Di was placed on the settee and I spent the night on the floor, next to her.

The next week raced past or crept with infinite slowness. I dunno. It was a time devoid of belief that what was happening was real. It was as if I was the main character in a play I resented being in. Di went away and was returned to us to lie in an open coffin in front of the fireplace. But it was so obviously not her.

Rob and Wayne arrived. They'd been contacted via Di's sister Judith while awaiting their plane at Heathrow.

People poured in with food, flowers, love. Percy Kukatai brought a delegation from Tekohanga and spoke a karakia, the group sang a waiata and it was as if a door opened. For the first time since that awful evening, I cried.

Later Sally said she too had had an epiphany. She had encountered a living spiritual reality which was to affect the rest of her life.

On the day of the funeral we assembled in our brightest, most colourful clothes. Di and I had discussed this. Death was a transition; you didn't have to grieve; you were allowed to laugh, to remember, to celebrate. The general invitation explicitly stated 'colourful attire'. And people adhered to the request.

Percy said it was perfectly fine to carry Di to the Hall where the celebration of her life was to be held. So a group of us, growing as we went along carried the coffin, taking it in turns. The pre-school stood outside and sang 'Old Macdonald had a farm'; we cheered and clapped.

Inside there were speeches and songs and tears.

And we all returned to 631 Tekohanga Road while Di's body left for the Crematorium in Manukau.

There were many cards and many tributes. I think there's a pile somewhere unless they've been swept away in a general clean-up, but I wrote my own tribute in my Green poetry book and I'll close this part of my life by jotting it down.

To Di. Written 14 January, 2011

Where have those ten years gone
since last I wrote?
And now it's me with Hamlet and Spiff,
emails and telephone.

They disappeared in music, in colour
in five minutes one April evening,
With Sally and the girls and me aghast, numbed at
the suddenness of Di's leaving.
But thank you for the years, the journey we
shared,
the times we loved
And raged, and made ends meet.

The kids we raised, the dogs, the cats and chooks
and ducks, and Golly and Polly, an opossum,
our goats.
And our boats, Simone, Roanaki and Tess
And tramping and canoeing the tributaries

of the Waikato.
Planning different futures together.
Together, always together.
Tunnel houses, canoeing, health talks and music
Oh the bands.
Over the Hill, Hangar Torque, Patchwork.
Nights of music and campfires,
griddle-cake, school trips.
The home we built and shared with everyone
for comfort and chats and laughter and tears.
Singing and hugs at the pre-schools,
Lakeside and the aged.
And grand-daughters;
those albums full of memories you filled.
The colour of our home,
the yellows you loved and the reds and blues
and yellows of the garden you planted.

You were, are, my rock, the stability
from which I could leap and return without harm.

A couple of pages this, but it was fifty years.
A whole library written by you and by me.
Others know parts of the book,
but we know it all.
Sleep well, my darling Di.

Chapter Thirty two. 2010 - 2015

The district rallied around, cleaned up the section and sorted out Di's clothes. They sent a roomful of black plastic bags jammed with skirts and tops, and undies and overs, to the Islands. Rob and Sally ripped up the coconut matting, extinguishing countless species with a tsunami of devastating violence which ended in flames.

Life buzzed along at an even more frenzied rate, sweeping me into a whirlwind of activities.

Bridget entered my life when her younger daughter, Hillberry, asked me to be the male figure in her life at a meeting of the Tuakau Kea Group a few months after Di's death.

Some years earlier I'd seen Bridget walking her two Yorkshire terriers and had mentioned to Di that a new family was in the district with dogs like Tess. Also we had periodically encountered Hillberry at preschool music where, pondering on the gender of the short-haired, blue-eyed child clad in jeans, we asked it for a name.

'Hillberry.'

Which didn't help much.

I went along to Keas and within a few months was helping out at a Summer camp. January of the next year I agreed to join the Tuakau Sea Scout Group officially. Hillberry moved from Keas to join her sister Eadlin in the Cubs and Bridget became a Cub leader with me as an assistant. Although I'd not had much to do with scouting for years I had helped Donna Casey with Onewhero Keas once or twice, flying my now defunct parachutes, and I could remember my own days as a Cub and later as patrol-leader in the Roan School troop.

Rob and Wayne had decided to make New Zealand their home and remained in Onewhero until the commute to Auckland became too much and they rented a luxurious flat overlooking the harbour. When Bridget, two weeks after I'd agreed to help out at Cubs, disappeared for a six week holiday in the U.K. I was left in charge of about twenty 8 to 11 year old boys and girls. Fortunately Rob and Wayne helped.

'What're you doing this week?'

'Cave at Strang's.'

'Sounds okay; we'll come.'

That was the time I almost castrated myself on the rope I'd fed from the small cave down a slippery slope. I didn't quite remember how the rope went: over the shoulder, through the leg, back elsewhere.

'Shit Mike! That looks painful.'

No-one else used that method.

We'd also brought along Titch and Sapper, Bridget's two dogs I'd offered to look after.

'Where's Titch?'

And the expedition stopped while we searched the undergrowth.

Not quite knowing what the modern Cub curriculum was we did what we, Rob, Wayne and I thought we'd enjoy such as cooking on bonfires, treks and rafting. W'ed discovered a large pond in Onewhero owned by Pete's sister and her husband, and enjoyed evenings canoeing there.

Then Bridget returned and everything settled down. Her husband Paul, Dobsy to all his mates, had died in a motor-cycle crash racing in the TT on the Isle of Man two weeks after Di died. Many things brought us together. It started with Keas and scouting and, heaven help us, we both knew the words to Ginganggooly and the Woad song but we swiftly found many other interests in common – music, sports, sailing, canoeing, reading, mutual dislike for television and a preference for anything you did yourself compared to a spoon-fed life.

Admittedly she couldn't play cribbage but she had a friend who did.

She was/is thirty two years younger than I and although it did once pass through my mind that a relationship in the modern sense might evolve, it didn't. But a fairly deep friendship has survived both Aaron, whom she found on a dating site, and Bernadette with whom I have settled down in Tauranga.

Meantime I continued to coach girls' soccer at Onewhero, was, elevated to the position of Convenor for the Duke of Edinburgh Awards at the local schools which for a while included Tuakau as well as Onewhero, taught kids how to sail at Port Waikato and still helped out with the drama club.

In fact in 2011 I was nominated for some awards recognizing service to the youth in Franklin. Bridget accompanied me to the ceremony and urged me to join her at the Onewhero Fire station where there was a party. This was organized by another Donna who had sent around invitation via email to a Mike Carter Award celebration to everyone on her list. Which included me. So while Bridget persuaded me that the Fireman's Ball would be fun I felt obliged to pretend I was unaware of its actual intention. I managed to convince everyone I really hadn't opened my email 'I only look at them once or twice a week..' I didn't want people to feel disappointed. So I used all my dramatic skills to convince Bridget that I would attend her Fireman's thing despite being reluctant and tired, and everyone else by being totally surprised when I was greeted, just as someone who'd just found out people liked him would feel.

I'd drive the car to Pukekohe to do the week's shopping and the seat beside me was empty.

Not that I was ever lonely. Keith and Marilyn were a paddock away. They'd been part of our spiritual path with Henny. We shared a set of swings which had been carted from garden to garden as our children grew up, as grandchildren arrived. Now the swings are at 631, my place. It's a bit dilapidated but functioning, a phrase which admirably describes both the house and me.

For the record, 'now' is January 2019. Aaron's girl-friend Chrissy, whom he'd introduced into the house unbeknownst to me some years ago, now lives there.

Lady passing through kitchen en route to toilet, 'Hello, I'm with Aaron.'

Me, 'Hi. I'm Mike. I, ...er, own this place.'

'Yes. He told me.'

Chrissy appeared after Bridget and Aaron had split up. Aaron's daughter, Leah. Chrissy is currently renting 631. I've seen someone on the swings.

Dori often popped in, so did Ann. The Lorimor kids, Joe and Ruby and Liddy their dog, would arrive about four in the afternoon for biscuits and car-games. Petra, now a high-school beauty had long give up playing with the dinky-cars. She'd only appear to drag the others down for dinner. Richard still arrived on a Wednesday for music and later on John Dwen, one of Ralf's brothers, would stop in for a cuppa on his way from or to Pukekohe.

I still performed in Onewhero Society of Performing Arts productions although I preferred life in the chorus which mostly involved lustily singing a heap of songs. One could merely lip-sync when the lines were forgotten. There were always enthusiastic ladies whom you could depend on to know the lyrics.

On one occasions, after sixteen years, we repeated 'Androcles and the Lion' and I was again given the relatively lineless (not a deliberate pun) part of the latter. The worst moment saw me dangling from a pole carried by two peasants. I was conscious that the probability of it snapping, or one end slipping, was high.

Also I'd rediscovered the Port Waikato Sailing Club which Di and I had joined in the sixties but had left when the reality of fighting an ebbing tide meant the land slipped away ahead of us and we had to be towed home.

I came to appreciate that Australia wasn't really far away and made a point of fostering the happier association I had with Sally. My musical skills had increased as I started to learn all the songs Di and I had sung together at pre-schools and I went solo. Sometimes, in one of the lesser exclusive rest-homes in Australia, Sally let me play alongside her.

A primary school teacher at Onewhero, Molly, often joined me at a pre-school session there but I played at the Wise Owls pre-school by myself. Molly and her husband owned Mungo

And there were still the Cubs. Bridget and I would meet on a Monday night and, over a bottle of wine, prepare for the meeting on the following evening. There was a programme set out but we often amended it in the light of our own experiences and interests. Similar to the Duke of Edinburgh scheme, the Cub plan involved four cornerstones involving community work, personal skills – physical and mental - and outdoor ventures. We would list all the cubs and find what they needed to complete various awards.

If we discovered any discrepancies we'd be creative with the activity. Thus lighting a candle could be interpreted variously as a mental exercise displaying unique emotional skills, a community service illuminating darkness, an adventurous outdoor skill.

Tuesday we'd have the meeting, and in the evening return to Bridget's house to work out who'd done what. And another bottle of wine. There were also camps. Organising the cubs was a task involving heaps of work, energy and time. I did it for four years, Bridget, now a group leader, is still doing it. There are of course, rewards, knowing you've helped young people feel they've achieved something, sharing the exuberance of youth, rediscovering forgotten pleasures. We introduced them to parachuting; letting them inflate my old chutes and feel the strength and power of the wind.

We went on night walks around the Kaipo Flats or through the dunes at Port Waikato. There was one nasty moment when we mislaid six Cubs and an adult for half an hour. We swam in streams, slid down waterfalls, explored rock pools. Broke an arm. All great fun, but in some ways I was tiring of it, especially when Bridget moved to the Scouts and I found the other Cub leaders not as organized as I'd come to expect. The expected preliminary preparation of a glass of wine went west.

One of the last Cub camps I attended was at Birkenhead on the North Shore in Nov 2014. I'd I had my car stolen from there; contents gone too, which included my wallet and cheque book.

The car was found, a bit battered, but my credit cards and cheque book had been used. I discovered this whilst shopping discovering to my horror that my card was rejected being $17000 overdrawn. This was somewhat staggering as I'd already contacted the bank to stop the cards and so forth but the thieves had beaten them to the draw. Anyway, things worked out okay. The car was repaired and I still own her, accounts were honoured. However, on 12 Dec 2018 someone used one of those old cheques to forge my name and draw out $870.

I had to consult diaries then to find the relative police reports, until finally the $870 was refunded.

Chapter Thirty three

At the other end of the age spectrum, June McCoubrie persuaded me to take on the role of stage manager for the Franklin Ageing Expo which I filled from 2010 to 2016. This involved monthly meetings in Pukekohe, assembling enough entertainments to fill in morning and afternoon sessions and assuring that the entertainers knew when to arrive.

It was an interesting position. Various arguments had to be settled – should the belly-dancers share a dressing room with the ladies presenting aged fashion? As there was only one dressing-room this was tricky. Timetables had to be juggled, always bearing in mind no-one wanted an afternoon slot.... And if for example, the Philippino drummers were given an unexpected encore, whose slot would be shortened? The opening was also an occasion of heart-searching.

Tables, free-standing signage boards lighting and the sound system were set up on the day preceding the Expo but the stall-owners themselves, although encouraged to prepare earlier, usually arrived less than an hour before the official 9 o'clock start.

The doors were opened at 9 a.m. with the honoured guests walking to their seats on the stage being welcomed by a powhiri provided by a local bus-driver who had access to a school haka-group.

This was done to the accompaniment of the audience arriving, the final stalls being set-up and the various offerings being admired, a loud hum drowning the platitudes from the microphone.

It was unsatisfactory and when the bus driver made himself unavailable, the local Maori cop when being tentatively asked to officiate made it clear that he resented a) being assigned a ten minute slot b) the blatant tokenism and c) the background noise. He'd been to a previous Expo.

'A Maori welcome is trivialising and unnecessary. All you're doing is pandering to the pc element who think they're doing the right thing.'

'I agree.' I'd reached that conclusion myself.

So in 2015 I got in touch with the local Pukekohe pipe band who refused to provide a piper without a considerable amount of money being donated, and then heard of a piping lady in Onewhero.

She and her daughter opened the 2015 and 2016 Expositions with a blare of highland pipes that stilled the hum. Visitors followed the pipers onto the stage.

'I declare this Expo open.'

The pipes broke into a highland fling and the day was started.

Wonderful.

I don't know if the Expo still survives. I hope so. I found it enjoyable and instructive. The stalls, almost ninety of them, ran through the gamut of activities and problems that the aged suffer plus quilting, cards, banking, welfare, sports, deafness, bowls,

I watched fascinated as Chris, who was the man who ran the whole affair, settled a dispute between a local bowling club who had booked a table and the local bowling association who thought they had. There were almost blows before Chris organized another table.

Free food was on offer. It attracted, justifiably – and I'm not only writing about the food – people of all ages.

And as for the entertainment. I prided myself on adding performing dogs and a young pre-school choir to the collection of dancers, singers, drummers, karate exponents and tai-chi exponents I'd inherited.

The belly-dancers were the greatest pulling card. As they swept on stage with magnificent costumes, bare midriffs and mind-numbing hip movements, the Expo became silent. It was a totally eye-boggling scene.

However, a serious duty of the committee demanded that we collect free prizes to present to the swarm of visitors who flooded in, which entailed traipsing along the retail outlets seeking donations. I was always surprised at how generous and understanding most were. Often however this meant calling back later and having to make copious notes to prevent repeating the same spiel to someone who'd heard it the previous week.

Bridget didn't keep Aaron secret. She introduced him to the district at a concert held in the Morris' garden. The affair lasted about six months during which she encouraged me to find myself a partner using a dating site.

Which sort of brings me to sex.

Yes, I did find soft porn sites on the internet. Yes, I did avail myself of the escort agency in Pukekohe called 'King's Arcade' where I was introduced to two girls and although one suggested I could try both simultaneously I settled for one.

'It's been almost two years, since my wife died,' I told her.

She commiserated. But I couldn't perform. We lay there. She tried. I tried. She was very kind, very understanding. 'It's just not working,' I muttered.

'Try the sauna.'

But I knew that wouldn't help. I think I needed real affection, not bought at $160 an hour no matter how good the actress.

'I'm sorry,' she said.

'Not your fault.'

The second time, this occasion at Manukau, the result was the same, Again the girl apologised. She let me talk. And I gave her an extra $20 for the bra cup by the bed.

'There's no need, honestly.'

It seemed that either my body really was getting too old for sex – which an experiment showed it wasn't - or I'd better find someone I could have a genuine attachment to. So I signed up to an on-line dating site.

There were three ladies before Bernadette each an interesting interlude in the on-going round of Onewhero life.

Lori I met outside the Hollywood in Manukau. We met a couple of times at her house. She played a guitar and owned an identical coloured Mazda Demio. Good start, but essentially she was searching for someone who shared an interest in cruise liners and exotic places; and could possibly pay for them. And my dress sense was not up to expectation.

So, Anne. She lived in Hamilton and we met at a restaurant just outside of Huntley opposite the now defunct powerhouse on the other side of the Waikato, drank coffee and decided to meet again. She came to Onewhero, where we slept in different rooms.

She listened to Rita Cary and me as we played an arrangement of 'Summertime' which we later put on at the 2014 Matariki Festival in the Onewhero Theatre. She approved. We went for a walk along Harker's Reserve where she told me of her prowess in speed walking and how she could circumnavigate the Hamilton Lake without a pause.

I also stayed at her house overnight, in separate rooms and was introduced to the widower next door who was a good keen gardener. I subtlety suggested she'd be better suited to someone living closer and we parted, amiably enough but without any arrangements for further meetings.

Adele I met at a café in Taupiri. We chatted. She'd had an accident and limped badly, spoke gently and told me shyly of the coarse jokes made by her female friends in the working men's club to which she belonged. She later sent me an email saying the cup of coffee we'd had together was the nicest she'd ever had.

I replied saying I'd also enjoyed meeting her but ... I can't remember the 'but' bit.

Then I arranged to meet up with Bernadette at Raglan; we walked along the beach holding hands. We had the obligatory cup of coffee. A week or so later she flew to England for a month's holiday during which time we emailed each other regularly. We clicked and here we are.

Bernadette is about my height, has been married and divorced. She was a social worker, and was renting a house in Cambridge in the Waikato. Many of her family scattered abroad: in England, Vietnam and Australia. A son and granddaughter lived in New Zealand.

She's a fiercely independently-minded woman with an almost obsessive (she dislikes this word) compulsion for having a place for everything and everything in its place. It says much for the forbearance, tolerance and love we have towards each other that we're still happily together.

Funny thing that word love. It means different things, like Eskimos describing snow, at different times, different ages. We share a house, meals, conversations about the news, shopping expeditions, a bed, silences, families, and holidays. There's a great deal of sharing as the house gets cleaned, the meals are cooked, the yard swept. It's a functioning companionship. Another sort of love.

I started visiting Cambridge, and later Rototuna, stopping weekends and extending this to three or four days until ultimately we moved to Tauranga. She made it clear that the haphazard life of Onewhero and the hundred year old house it involved was not something she could cope with. Over the last few years, living in houses possessing central heating, with minimal lawns, immaculate furnishings, served by someone who enjoyed cooking....what can I say?

In 2014 I resigned from Cubs, gave up coaching girls' soccer and handed over the reins of Duke of Ed convener to Bridget.

Discovering Lake Kaituna, close to Rototuna, I brought down a couple of canoes and a Starling sailing dinghy and the transition was completed when I fetched down my flying machine - now powered by a brand new Rotax 503 engine with a three bladed prop – and deposited him at Martin Hindley's airstrip in Gordonton. Incidentally I've always had a dilemma about the gender of my flying machine. Now it's in writing. Male.

It was during the Rototuna years that I cemented in my morning exercise regime. Firstly there was trampoline bouncing in the garage, gradually coming to include arm and neck movements, Then a series of expeditions around the reserves and roads where I became familiar with the area – the road names reflecting a solidly English heritage; Wentworth, Whitby, Whitechapel. Yet the main icon was a circle of Maori statues and a huge net depicting 'tuna', whitebait.

I've performed a variation of this routine every morning for the past twenty- odd years.

By 2015 Aaron was ensconced with his daughter, Leah, in my Onewhero house and when I moved out full-time, he started paying rent officially. Up until then it had been a random arrangement where we sort of shared costs. I get on well with Aaron who still periodically sends me video clips of his hang-gliding activities to which Bridget had introduced him in the days when they were an entity. (She'd been an enthusiastic hang-glider pilot in England but now feels an obligation to her daughters not to push limits).

Life was a mixture of Rototuna and Onewhero.

Two canoeing events stand out.

Bridget asked me to look after the girls for a couple of days. Not until later did I discover she'd rolled and written off Aaron's car and emotions were strained.

'Right. How about I take them over to that island opposite Carey's and we camp there a couple of days?'

'Anywhere you like.

I rang Percy Kukutai as the official local Kaumatua and he seemed surprised I'd bothered to ask but said that he'd tell someone we were coming. Actually there were a couple of dilapidated heaps of tin in which someone was reputed to be living but when we arrived by canoe the island was almost virginal. Some large kahikateas were surrounded by willows, manuka further in. There were swathes of stinging nettle, occasional clumps of inkweed, wild blackberry even an occasional patch of grass. On a high tide we entered a small bay and landed on a muddy beach.

'Find a camp site,' I told the girls.' I'll unload the canoe.' We'd brought along an Explorer – a double-seated Canadian design – and it was full with the necessities of island life. I paddled this with Hillberry and Eadlin in single canoes.

'It's 'Swallows and Amazons,' said Eady as they disappeared into the undergrowth.

Apart from a controversy involving mud and me telling them I'd take them back to Bridget, if it wasn't settled 'RIGHT NOW,' it was an idyllic three days. We explored the island, finding signs of occupation and climbing up a precarious ladder to look over to Carey's settlement about fifty metres away on the mainland.

My navigational skills are not the greatest and in our inaugural ramble I'd taken no notice of direction believing that it would be impossible to get lost...I suddenly realized that we were, and my safest option of returning was to follow the edge of the island until we reached our little muddy bay. Rather than confess my ineptitude a sudden, cunning alternative popped into my head.

'Take it in turns to lead us back. You first, Hillberry.'

'It's this way until we hit that blackberry bush. Bush corner,' she added, making it sound obvious

'Jolly good,' I murmured approvingly.

'Look that's the watering place by the small pool.'

'And there's the 'Hidden hole.''

'The tall tree's next.'

Tall tree? What the hell were they talking about?

But then we pushed our way through some toetoe grass and saw the tents.

'Ah...well done.'

Thinking of Bridget's daughters I will mention another incident involving a sibling disagreement. I call it:

Chapter Thirty four.
The Shortening of the Wizard's Wand

The waterfall at Mitchells is named either Vivien Falls or Te Heke o Maui depending who's listening and I'd often wondered on its actual course as it wended its way to the Waikato. Percy once delivered a blessing there and boards in Maori and English tell the story, also explaining the name of the area, Kaipo Flats, from which the water flowed. In our first months in New Zealand, back in 1962, Di and I had run out of tank water and would drive there after school to have a natural cold shower under the stream of frothing water tumbling down.

We were oblivious that much of the effluent of surrounding farms poured into the stream as it meandered through the Kaipo Flats before disappearing over the thirty foot fall. I'd once abseiled down its face, attaching one end of the rope to a stake and watched by a Maori lass, Carolyn Rau, with whose family we were quite friendly.

Anyway, I suggested to Eady and Hillbberry an expedition following the stream until it reached the Waikato.

We started at the foot of the waterfall, resisting the temptation it offered to slide along the wall behind the curtain of spray, and set off following the bank unless the rocks midstream looked more interesting.

Amongst the undergrowth Hillberry discovered a magic wand. To the casual observers. i.e. Eady or me, it looked like an ordinary twig but Hillberry assured us it possessed magic qualities and waved it in complicated patterns to keep us clear of misfortune.

Shortly afterwards the banks became vertical and we chose to walk through the water, with Hillberry walking ahead incantenting and wafting off evil.

The depth of the water increased, reaching our waists and Hillberry stopped.

'We can get round if we grab those roots,' pointed out Eady, indicating a tree clinging to the bank. Look.' And she stepped forward, clasping onto the roots until she clambered onto a convenient rock.

'I'll help you,' I told Hillberry who was watching the swirling water with a worried expression. 'Just pass me the wand,' I added as she hesitated.

She handed me the stick and I passed it on to Eady while, standing up to my chest in water and steadying Hillberry as she felt her way towards her sister.

Gratefully we reached shallower water. 'I'll have the wand now,' said Hillberry. Then she let out a screech.

The wand had dramatically halved its length.

'You broke it,' she accused Eady.

'It must have used up its magic getting us round that bank,' replied Eady. It was an unconvincing and, to Hillberry, an unsatisfying explanation although I thought it at eminently creative. However I made Eady apologise before I allowed her to have some of the toilet paper I'd brought with me when she suddenly had to make a dash for the nearest bush.

The other canoeing incident merits a name but lacks one as it still irritates me. It involves Bernadette. I first went canoeing with Bernadette when Rob brought

Pauline, his team leader at Tower, her husband John and their family of five to stop overnight at our place.

That had been a great occasion, one of the highlights being when the ten year-old, Larry, was handed a mini-motorbike owned by Joe who was the son of our next door neighbour, Scott.

It eventuated that Larry hadn't really been instructed, merely let loose and he ended up riding through a tent. Bridget was appalled when she heard of the event.

'Totally irresponsible,' she chided, 'Scott's lucky nothing really nasty occurred.'

I reminded her of this a couple of weeks later when she had Joe in a Sunburst sailing dinghy at the Port. Aaron was with Eady in another Sunny and I and Hillberry were in an Optimist when we observed firstly, Joe and Bridget swimming around their capsized boat, and then Aaron heading for and colliding with, the beach. Seems his forestay had pulled out so this was excusable but the capsized dinghy was attributable to Joe's steering into an unexpected jibe about which he had not been warned.

'Easy to think kids know more than they do,' I murmured as we discussed the day over glasses of wine. 'Scott had a similar problem.' We left it at that.

More about Bernadette's canoeing activities. The first was with Rob's mob when we took them all canoeing around Carey's island. It was a fine and successful day. We have a photograph of a laughing Bernadette on our fridge door being helped by Wayne to squeeze into the narrow canoe. A great and memorable day. The latter adjective not having its usual connotation of something recalled with a momentous shudder.

The next occasion for Bernadette to try out a canoe was on Lake Kaituna outside Rototuna. Despite her excellent performance on the Waikato, she was a reluctant starter and only agreed when Tony, her son accompanied her; he sat in the rear seat of the Canadian with his mother up front. Becky, Tony's daughter had a minnow and I paddled a slim dura.

We reached what looked like a possible landing spot but I thought there might be one with a safer place just around a point further along. 'Hang on here,' I said, 'until I have a look. Then we'll land and have something to eat.' I didn't want anything wet to happen.

Then I shot off to prospect for a suitable picnic spot. When I returned it was to a party on shore with a dripping Bernadette foreswearing anything further to do with canoes.

'What happened?' I asked.

Becky had gone ashore first. She'd stood on the bank and offered her grandmother a helping hand from the canoe. Bernadette stepped ashore being hauled up alongside Becky who was standing next to a grass-covered hole in the bank. She's not canoed since

We settled into the routine of Friday, Saturday and Sunday at Rototuna, the rest of the week in Onewhero. I enjoyed the three days at Rototuna for the peace. It gives a welcome break from the inrush of visitors, the hectic round of drama, music, mowing, chopping, and shopping.

I even came to look forward to the television programmes – Midsommer Murders with the background of rural England, and Jack Frost – David Jason keeping London safe. I eventually moved to Rototuna fulltime, even bringing my flying machine, which I flew from a lay heavyfarmer's strip in Gordonton. Pete Hinley owned a Bantam 22 and once took me up in it for an instructive half hour.

I had a salutary lesson one wintry morn when a heavy dew lay all around. The canopy didn't rise cleanly and one tip dragged on the ground. I kept going hoping it would catch the wind. What it did was slew sideways into the prop which neatly sliced two lines.

The next flight would be a couple of months hence in Waihi.

Bernadette's work had brought her into contact with an Indian family living close, immigrants like us. The daughter and son were determined to be good kiwis and Ashita refused to speak Hindi. I admired the family and the common-sense of the parents not to make a big deal of this.

They visited us in Tauranga, and I stayed overnight at their house a couple of times when Bernadette was having an operation. One of these almost cost her life.

Other immigrants, Muslim and Hindu, invited us to their homes and parties. It brought home the eclectic nature of New Zealand society which had not been so obvious in Onewhero. We lived together for some months in Rototuna.

In December 2015 we spent over a week in a small hired bach in Doubtless Bay. It was divided into two parts, which involved having to cook and live in one area and crossing over to another room to go to bed. Still, even if Christmas lunch was a roast cooked at the beach in a portable BBQ, I was learning that holidays didn't have to entail sleeping under canvas or squashed up in a boat. I was learning to spend money, something I've always been careful to avoid.

Bernadette's lease on the Rototuna house ran out in July and we decided to move somewhere closer to the sea.

We drove to Tauranga and, using a room in the house of Reece, a friend of Tony's, as a base, explored the Bay of Plenty area. Finally we decided to rent a house overlooking the golf course in Mount Maunganui, and we moved in July, 2016.

This has been our home since. It is a seven minute walk to the beach in one direction, and about the same distance to Bayfair which is our local shopping mall. It vies with Sylvia Park in Auckland for size and entertainment.

Two years have passed, and Bernadette and I look back over two years here together.

Chapter Thirty five.
The present 2016 - 2019

Which brings everything, interestingly, to about now. We rented a house in a quiet road ending in a reserve boasting the purity of its non-toxic environment. Our lounge overlooks the golf course and from the kitchen window we can see the reserve which starts barely ten metres from our front door.

Bayfair Mall was large when we arrived and now is considerably even more extensive. I wondered at first if I could hear the sea but on reflection, this background noise could well be the stream of traffic pouring down Ocean Beach Road which separates the reserve from the dunes. However, the very volume of traffic conspires to inhibit its speed so crossing the road to reach the beach is not a fearsome task.

Neither of our families are really close so a weekly family gathering doesn't come about. We're glad if Tony pops in. He usually brings a meal, or Becky. Rob and Wayne have spent a couple of days, Bridget and the girls ditto, Sally has spent a week here and so has Josephine and her boy-friend, Ryan. Sophie and Bonnie came with Sally once.

Periodically I visit Onewhero, leaving Tauranga about 7.00 am on a Friday so I can have a music session with Richard before meeting everyone else. After the obligatory coffee and cake I cruise around Onewhero, casting an eye on the house and picking up music or bits of paper or tools before catching up on John Dwen, Bridget, Keith and Marilyn before descending on Rob and Wayne for chats and a bed.

It is like visiting a different world and the three hour journey, broken by a stop for coffee at Ngatea emphasizes the transition.

Bernadette has dragged me off to various clothing and shoes stores where attire more suited to her requirements have been purchased.

We have also had an exotic holiday in Samoa. That was April/May 2017. We were moved from a room in a hotel into a grass-roofed fale just alongside the sea where we rested and ate and luxuriated in served meals. There was a pool with a bar in the middle, and as much ocean as we wanted. I spent a day in Apia travelling thither on a smallish local bus which at its destination in town disgorged itself of (I counted) 72 persons.

We'd have a pre-dinner with 'The Captain', we'd have drinks with the meal and, I'm sure, but wouldn't swear to it, a post-prandial swig too. I found I enjoyed coconut milk which is non- alcoholic, and all in all we had a great time there. We got on well with the staff who seemed surprised and pleased that I'd had survived the local bus. One of them took us to another resort where there was a concert party, and we were invited to a rehearsal of a performance at our resort due the day after we were leaving.

The 2016 Expo was my last one. I presented Chris with a list of all my contacts and am unsure who inherited the task. Having ditched scouting, girls' soccer and OSPA, apart from being a spectator, I determined on a hedonistic existence devoid of responsibilities other than those involving Bernadette and myself. Life at Mount Maunganui is possessed of an air of perpetual holiday.

Early appreciating that a full enjoyment of the situation would involve a certain level of fitness, I continue to commence each day with exercise; trampoline, push-ups. I can now manage fifty push-ups; yoga stretches, and a quiet period of contemplation. I write a diary and have re-read through many of the years I made vain attempts to gain some insight into the meaning of my existence. You're welcome to try but even I find the 'calligraphy' daunting.

Each morning I read the daily meditation. If you ignore lots of the 'Christ Consciousness' and 'Beloved Presence of God' bits, I reckon there's a good deal of common sense.

Finally, before breakfast I walk along the beach usually with a dog. Dogs? Oh, yes. Mungo belonged to Molly and Martin. He was a large mastiff whose presence gave off an incredible aura of pent-up savagery. He was in fact one of the most amiable hounds I've met. Molly used to bring him round a couple of days a week as he enjoyed company and both she and her husband were teaching.

She'd push the front door open and yell, 'Are you ready?'

'Yep.'

She'd let go of his collar (Mungo's, not Martin's): there'd a pounding of feet and into the room would hurtle Mungo, his feet scrabbling desperately on the wooden floor. He invariably skidded into the bar. Anyone in his path was sent sprawling. Bonnie loved him.

Di once told me, 'When I was in hospital, or feeling down in the dumps, I'd take the journey from school to home. Out of the school, past the old Post-office. Then down the hill and over the bridge, where the motor-bike once burst into flames and you scooped water out of the stream in a gum-boot, and then up to the first gate with the cows being sent down the race for milking. This was the same race where I got swept off back Trixie's back when she went under a low branch. There's another gate, then into our place greeted by a couple of goats.'

Me? I walk across a green reserve avoiding the cones in the grass. Then I peer up and down the road seeking a gap in the traffic before walking down to Beach Access 5.8 and a walk along a grassy stretch until suddenly I'm standing on a dune and the sky is vast and the sea stretches out to America. Sometimes there's Louie, the neighbour's dog and admittedly, sometimes there's a fierce cold wind and the sea is a grey mottled with foam. But my mind seems to expand.

I met Robert at a Welcome Bay fourth Sunday in the month Music club. It consisted of twelve concertino players and played a variety of old-tyme tunes to an appreciative but fairly aged audience. Neither Robert's ukulele nor my mandolin could compete although my recorder could make itself heard.

'I'm giving this away,' he muttered. We were given a spot to show our stuff but didn't make much of an impact. However I did learn of the Ukulele group meeting at Cliff Road each Monday afternoon and decided to join it.

Robert was in charge of chairs and tea and there being a dearth of other men, possibly three with twenty or so ladies completing the group. I offered to help him. Shortly afterwards he went on holiday and by the time he returned I found I was permanent tea-boy. This has not proved an onerous commitment although I am contemplating shifting the tea-pot responsibility onto a new arrival, Terry.

However, Terry is a retired lawyer and well able to avoid it. He is one of the very few men I've met of my own diminutive stature and we enjoy making tea together. The ladies genially and gratefully call us 'the boys.'

Reg organizes an Acoustic Group on Wednesdays which both Terry and I attend. Reg thought acoustic meant stringed but allows me to play my recorder and Blues harp. It's improved my ability to play by ear enormously.

To some extent I'm looked upon, quite erroneously, as a musical guru able to knock tunes out on mandolin, mouth-organ, recorder and ukulele. Sally shudders when I tell her this. Periodically she arrives over here and we go to the open mic night in the Pap House, the Papamoa pub, where she has a band of appreciative followers always asking me when she'll be back to dazzle them with her fiddle playing.

Music is a great therapy; it can be played solo or in a group, and calls on mental, physical and emotional inputs. And to reach an acceptable standard you don't have to be a virtuoso – all it takes is the desire to play the instrument you've chosen and the willingness to practice it.

Chapter Thirty six. And more

It's been a tough few years for Bernadette. She gave up full-time work when we left Rototuna and has spent much of the time since in pain. She's had a major operation to clear an artery in her neck and shortly afterwards a hip replacement. There was talk at one time of having a specialist at the head end and one further down while an anesthetist monitored progress but the operations were performed consecutively over a couple of months. Then she went to England for three months where she tripped over a step and bust her fibula. A rod was inserted and screwed into place. It is this which causes the pain. Hopefully it will be remedied early this year (now 2019).

Despite all of this we've had holidays where considerable amounts of money was expended, something I've not really been accustomed to doing. My idea of a holiday was one involving mountains or small boats, tents or minute cabins, heaps of sweat and smokey fires. Bernadette has taught me there are possibly, even to me, more pleasant alternatives.

We have rented houses at Doubtless Bay and Henderson Bay. We had a small self-contained Bure in Samoa, we've toured the South West area of Australia in a hired car stopping at motels and eating at restaurants. Admittedly, at Margaret River I did buy a meat pie and heated it in the microwave oven we found in the kitchen. And we regularly, well, always, have wine with our meal.

My clothing sense has remained incorrigibly op-shop so Bernadette now buys everything I need from more fashionable outlets.

I've been reading the last couple of years' diaries and occasionally come across comments questioning the likelihood of us still being together the following month, or year.

Well, we are and there's no real reason why things won't stay that way until either I'm sprinkled over Onewhero or Bernadette becomes a medical specimen.

So here I am, reasonably up to date. I've missed out odd bits such as the tramp up Egmont with Rob and Bridget, and the Abel Tasman National Park walk.

There've been visits from relatives, both mine and Bernadette's, and we've shown them the sights of Tauranga and the Mount.

The flying side has come to an abrupt halt. A wire broke, the front wheel dug into a soft bit of airstrip and everything crumpled forward. Except me. Am unsure whether I'll fix it.

But life is good.

Epilogue

I'm stumped for words; doesn't happen often. I reckon I've said it all.

Perhaps I'll go straight to composing my own epitaph although someone else must do the recording. There are many famous final words....'Bloody doctors' ....'Wonder if this is safe?'....'Are you sure you know what you're doing?' And most pithy of all....'Oh, shit', as calamity becomes inevitable. That would be the way to go.

None of this hanging about with wires and tubes, wondering which bugger isn't going to visit. Still if that's ahead, may I be reconciled. May I lie down quietly and reminisce. Sort of drift away. Who wants visitors when there's so many things worth thinking about?

Unless I've forgotten them, of course.

I've always said, 'If in doubt, do it. Do it now!' I knew there was a reason for sharing my story.

Good night. March 2019

Printed in Great Britain
by Amazon